THE TECHNIQUE OF CANON

THE TECHNIQUE OF CANON

BY
HUGO NORDEN

Boston
BRANDEN PRESS
Publishers

Standard Book Number 8283-1028-9
© Copyright, 1970, by Branden Press, Inc.
Printed in the United States of America
Library of Congress Catalog Card Number 69-17504

To my wife, Mary

FOREWORD

The present slim volume has a single specific objective: namely, to set forth simply and concisely the principles of canon writing. The concern is exclusively with the mechanics of this highly specialized branch of musical composition, and not with its historical development. Thus, the few classical examples that are included are examined on this basis.

This book is extracted from a much larger and far more comprehensive treatise on canon which remains unpublished. Consequently, vastly more can be said about the artistic application of the structural principles of canon than is contained herein, but the principles as such are complete as given.

The conventional exercises that usually follow each chapter in most textbooks on music theory are here intentionally omitted. It seems more realistic and fruitful for the student or his teacher to set up original problems for each type of canon and thereby employ the principles more creatively.

HUGO NORDEN

Boston, Massachusetts

CONTENTS

INTRODUCTION

THE DOUBLE COUNTERPOINT PRINCIPLE

1.   Canon derives its musical nature as well as its structural being from the utilization and manipulation of Double Counterpoint. Therefore, before embarking upon the study of Canon itself, it is necessary to understand and master in every detail the whole principle and the practical mechanics of Double Counterpoint.

2.   In its most elementary form Double Counterpoint means that two complementary themes that are intended for simultaneous performance are so written that either one can correctly serve as bass to the other. By identifying two such complementary themes as 'I' and 'II' respectively, a Double Counterpoint mechanism can be operative as follows:

Ex. 1

(a)

(b)

The method involved is that of vertical displacement. It can be seen at a glance from the following illustration on three staves how II is shifted downward one octave from its position above I to a new relationship below I.

Ex. 2

It can, of course, be argued that II is shifted an octave upward from below I to function above it.

3.   Such a double counterpoint structure is always identified according to the interval of the vertical displacement; the present case being Double Counterpoint at the 8ve, hereafter to be abbreviated simply as D. C. 8.

4.   A practical illustration of an invertible two-part structure of this type, but in a somewhat more elaborate form, is found at the beginning of Bach's Invention No. 6 in E major. It will be observed that the themes in measures 5 – 8 are exactly the same as those in measures 1 – 4, except that the vertical arrangement is shifted from $\frac{I}{II}$ to $\frac{II}{I}$.

12

Later in the Invention, measures 21 – 28, the same themes are used in the same way in the key of B major, but with the presentation reversed so that $\frac{II}{I}$ precedes $\frac{I}{II}$.

Ex. 4

Ex. 3 and 4 operate within D. C. 22, or D. C. 8 expanded by two octaves.

5.   In the preceding illustrations the two vertical arrange-
ments, $\frac{I}{II}$ and $\frac{II}{I}$ (vice versa in Ex. 4), appear contiguously
and in the same key. This is not always the case. In Ex. 5
(two passages from The Well-Tempered Clavier by Bach),
(a), measures 3 – 4, is in B minor while in (b), measures
22 – 23, the inversion is in E minor. The following quota-
tions are from Fugue X in Vol. 1.

Ex. 5

Because in a fugue the subject and answer are customarily given more prominence than the countersubject, in the above pair of illustrations the former are designated as 'I' and the latter as 'II'. However, from the purely mechanical considerations the I and II designations could be reversed with no effect upon the double counterpoint.

6.   All of the illustrations given above have demonstrated D. C. 8 or its expansion by two additional octaves into D. C. 22. Other intervals of inversion are equally possible and just as useful. They are, however, not so often encountered. Ex. 6 provides an instance of D. C. 7 and its resulting two-part structures.

Ex. 6

16

When the interval of vertical displacement is something other than D. C. 8, the inversion may require accidentals that will put it in a key different from that of the original. Such a tonality change is demonstrated in the $\frac{I}{II}$ arrangement above.

7. It is not necessary for the vertical displacement of one theme to be *from* above *to* below the other, or vice versa. That is to say, in a given $\frac{I}{II}$ contrapuntal structure I may be shifted up or down to another pitch above II; or, likewise, II may be shifted up or down to another pitch below I. Ex. 7 illustrates how such a shift can operate. The interval of vertical displacement is a 2nd upward, thereby bringing into play D. C. 2.

Ex. 7

17

From analysis of passages such as the above it would be impossible to tell in which direction the shift had been made. While it is stated that the displacement of I is upward away from the position closer to II, it could just as well be interpreted that I is shifted downward from the higher position towards II. Only the composer can be entirely certain as to the direction of the displacement.

8.   When the counterpoint and its displacement are both on the same side of the other theme as in the preceding illustration, the closer position of the two themes must be calculated in terms of minus (−) intervals. Minus intervals come about when the parts cross. While there appears

18

to be not the slightest evidence of any crossing of parts in Ex. 7, the following presentation of D. C. 2 on three staves shows why such a calculation in terms of minus intervals is necessary.

Ex. 8

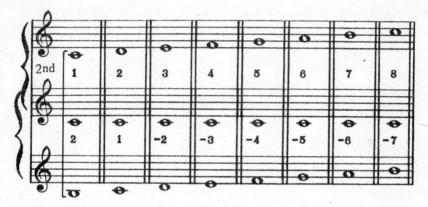

9. These introductory observations demonstrate the Double Counterpoint principle in its most obvious and elementary form. Actually, its application in the construction of canons is somewhat different and considerably more sophisticated. The remainder of the present volume will show these principles in operation in complete detail.

CHAPTER I

DOUBLE COUNTERPOINT

1.   A technique in Double Counterpoint within the diatonic system requires the mastery of seven basic intervals of inversion: D. C. 8, D. C. 9, D. C. 10, D. C. 11, D. C. 12, D. C. 13 and D. C. 14. Any other inversions that are necessary for systematic canon construction can be readily formulated by contracting or by expanding the above named inversions by an octave. The following three illustrations show how such adjustments are made.

2.   Take, for example, D. C. 10:

Ex. 9

This is expandable into D. C. 17 (10 + 8) by writing the counterpoint on the uppermost staff one octave higher:

Ex. 10

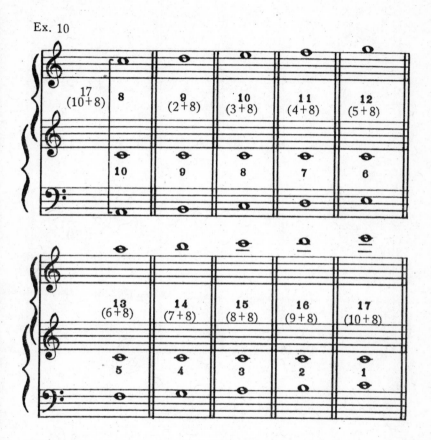

By the opposite method the interval of inversion can be compressed to D. C. 3 (10–8) by writing the counterpoint on the lowest staff of Ex. 9 one octave higher:

21

Ex. 11

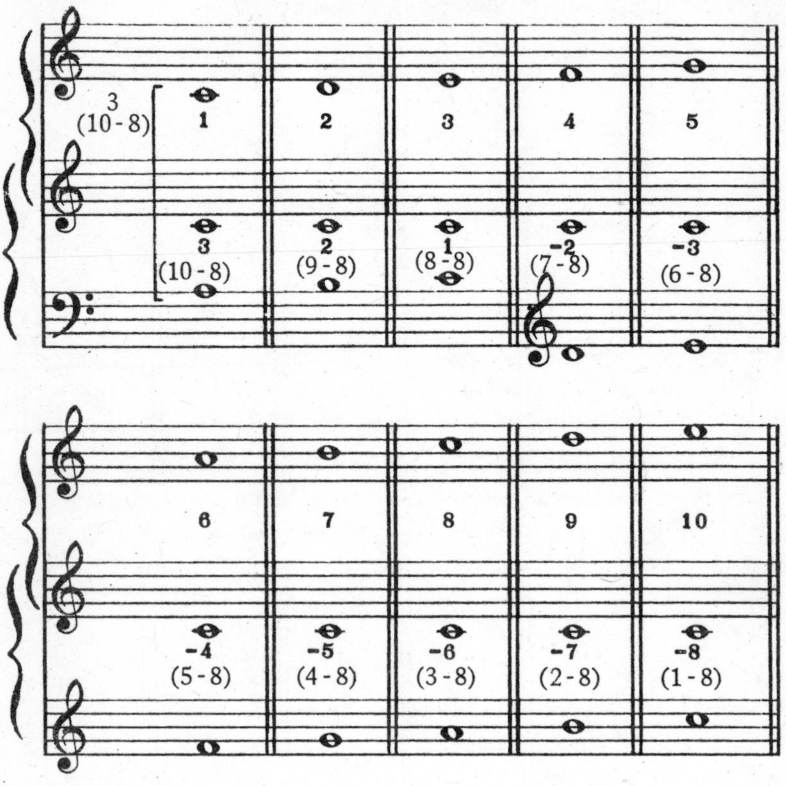

From the foregoing the following inversion relationships can be developed:

D. C. 8 = D. C. 15 (8 + 8), D. C. 1 (8–8)
D. C. 9 = D. C. 16 (9 + 8), D. C. 2 (9–8)
D. C. 10 = D. C. 17 (10 + 8), D. C. 3 (10–8)
D. C. 11 = D. C. 18 (11 + 8), D. C. 4 (11–8)
D. C. 12 = D. C. 19 (12 + 8), D. C. 5 (12–8)
D. C. 13 = D. C. 20 (13 + 8), D. C. 6 (13–8)
D. C. 14 = D. C. 21 (14 + 8), D. C. 7 (14–8)

22

Further octave expansions are likewise possible:

D. C. 15 + 8 = D. C. 22 (cf. Ex. 3, 4, and 5)
D. C. 16 + 8 = D. C. 23
D. C. 17 + 8 = D. C. 24
D. C. 18 + 8 = D. C. 25
D. C. 19 + 8 = D. C. 26
etc.

3. A word of explanation about the apparently strange arithmetic may be in order. Due to our system of numerical identification of intervals, when two intervals are added one note—the upper note of the lower interval and the lower note of the upper interval—is counted twice. And in the process of intervallic subtraction the same note is subtracted twice. The following diagram shows how this comes about.

Ex. 12

4. Each D. C. inversion must be studied separately for the particular concord-discord relationships it contains. What is shown below is in accordance with the traditional rules for correct academic counterpoint. This is provided merely as a frame of reference. Actually, the correctness of the counterpoint as such has nothing whatever to do with the arithmetical calculation of canons should a

composer's artistic intentions call for the construction of contrapuntal combinations quite outside the scope of traditional academic availabilities.

5.   In contrapuntal progression a tied note can result in three different situations:

> (1)   a correctly resolved suspension, indicated by S. ——> in the Table of Inversions;
>
> (2)   an incorrect suspension effect, indicated by Ṣ. ·····> ;
>
> (3)   a tie (i. e., a concord), indicated by T.·····>.

Resulting therefrom are nine inversion possibilities as follows:

(1) $\dfrac{\text{S.}\longrightarrow}{\text{S.}\longrightarrow}$	(4) $\dfrac{\text{Ṣ.}\cdots>}{\text{Ṣ.}\cdots>}$	(7) $\dfrac{\text{Ṣ.}\cdots>}{\text{T.}\cdots>}$
(2) $\dfrac{\text{S.}\longrightarrow}{\text{Ṣ.}\cdots>}$	(5) $\dfrac{\text{S.}\longrightarrow}{\text{T.}\cdots>}$	(8) $\dfrac{\text{T.}\cdots>}{\text{Ṣ.}\cdots>}$
(3) $\dfrac{\text{Ṣ.}\cdots>}{\text{S.}\longrightarrow}$	(6) $\dfrac{\text{T.}\cdots>}{\text{S.}\longrightarrow}$	(9) $\dfrac{\text{T.}\cdots>}{\text{T.}\cdots>}$

A corresponding set of illustrations in terms of 4th Species Counterpoint will demonstrate how the above combinations might appear in notation.

Ex. 13

25

*) Does not produce correct academic counterpoint.

**) Must be a correctly treated discord.

***) Double ties are not indicated on the Table of Inver-·
sions since no resolution problem exists.

6. Under certain conditions S.····→ can be changed
to S. ——→when the interval of inversion is expanded by
an octave. For instance, by expanding D. C. 8 to D. C. 15
the 2 – 1 effect in (4) above would become a correct 9 – 8
suspension.

Ex. 14

The expansion of the inversion does not improve the
academically faulty 7 – 8 effect below the Cantus Firmus.

7. The complete Table of Inversion follows.

26

D. C. 8:

$$\begin{array}{c} & & \text{S.} \rightarrow\text{S.} \rightarrow\text{T.} \cdots\rightarrow\text{S.} \rightarrow & & \text{S.} \cdots\rightarrow \\ \dfrac{8}{1} & \dfrac{7}{2} & \dfrac{6}{3} & \dfrac{5}{4*} & \dfrac{4*}{5} & \dfrac{3}{6} & \dfrac{2}{7} & \dfrac{1}{8} \\ & & \text{S.} \rightarrow\text{T.} \cdots\rightarrow\text{S.} \rightarrow\text{S.} \rightarrow & & \text{S.} \cdots\rightarrow \end{array}$$

D. C. 9:

$$\begin{array}{c} \text{S.} \rightarrow\text{T.} \cdots\rightarrow\text{S.} \rightarrow\text{S.} \rightarrow\text{T.} \cdots\rightarrow\text{S.} \rightarrow\text{T.} \cdots\rightarrow\text{S.} \cdots\rightarrow \\ \dfrac{9}{1} \quad \dfrac{8}{2} \quad \dfrac{7}{3} \quad \dfrac{6}{4*} \quad \dfrac{5}{5} \quad \dfrac{4*}{6} \quad \dfrac{3}{7} \quad \dfrac{2}{8} \quad \dfrac{1}{9} \\ \text{T.} \cdots\rightarrow\text{S.} \rightarrow\text{T.} \cdots\rightarrow\text{S.} \rightarrow\text{S.} \rightarrow\text{T.} \cdots\rightarrow\text{S.} \cdots\rightarrow\text{T.} \cdots\rightarrow \end{array}$$

D. C. 10:

$$\begin{array}{c} \text{S.} \rightarrow \qquad \text{S.} \rightarrow\text{S.} \rightarrow \qquad \text{S.} \rightarrow \qquad \text{S.} \cdots\rightarrow \\ \dfrac{10}{1} \quad \dfrac{9}{2} \quad \dfrac{8}{3} \quad \dfrac{7}{4*} \quad \dfrac{6}{5} \quad \dfrac{5}{6} \quad \dfrac{4*}{7} \quad \dfrac{3}{8} \quad \dfrac{2}{9} \quad \dfrac{1}{10} \\ \text{S.} \rightarrow \qquad \text{S.} \rightarrow\text{S.} \rightarrow \qquad \text{S.} \cdots\rightarrow \qquad \text{S.} \rightarrow \end{array}$$

D. C. 11:

$$\begin{array}{c} \text{S.} \rightarrow\text{T.} \cdots\rightarrow\text{S.} \rightarrow\text{T.} \cdots\rightarrow\text{S.} \rightarrow\text{S.} \rightarrow\text{T.} \cdots\rightarrow\text{S.} \rightarrow\text{T.} \cdots\rightarrow\text{S.} \cdots\rightarrow \\ \dfrac{11*}{1} \quad \dfrac{10}{2} \quad \dfrac{9}{3} \quad \dfrac{8}{4*} \quad \dfrac{7}{5} \quad \dfrac{6}{6} \quad \dfrac{5}{7} \quad \dfrac{4*}{8} \quad \dfrac{3}{9} \quad \dfrac{2}{10} \quad \dfrac{1}{11*} \\ \text{T.} \cdots\rightarrow\text{S.} \rightarrow\text{T.} \cdots\rightarrow\text{S.} \rightarrow\text{S.} \rightarrow\text{T.} \cdots\rightarrow\text{S.} \cdots\rightarrow\text{T.} \cdots\rightarrow\text{S.} \rightarrow\text{T.} \cdots\rightarrow \end{array}$$

D. C. 12:

$$\begin{array}{c} \text{S.} \rightarrow \qquad \text{S.} \rightarrow\text{T.} \cdots\rightarrow\text{S.} \rightarrow\text{S.} \rightarrow \qquad \text{S.} \rightarrow \qquad \text{S.} \cdots\rightarrow \\ \dfrac{12}{1} \quad \dfrac{11*}{2} \quad \dfrac{10}{3} \quad \dfrac{9}{4*} \quad \dfrac{8}{5} \quad \dfrac{7}{6} \quad \dfrac{6}{7} \quad \dfrac{5}{8} \quad \dfrac{4*}{9} \quad \dfrac{3}{10} \quad \dfrac{2}{11*} \quad \dfrac{1}{12} \\ \text{S.} \rightarrow \qquad \text{S.} \rightarrow\text{S.} \rightarrow\text{T.} \cdots\rightarrow\text{S.} \cdots\rightarrow \qquad \text{S.} \rightarrow \qquad \text{S.} \rightarrow \end{array}$$

D. C. 13:

$$\begin{array}{c} \text{S.} \rightarrow\text{T.} \cdots\rightarrow\text{S.} \rightarrow\text{T.} \cdots\rightarrow\text{S.} \rightarrow \qquad \text{S.} \rightarrow\text{S.} \rightarrow\text{T.} \cdots\rightarrow\text{S.} \rightarrow\text{T.} \cdots\rightarrow\text{S.} \cdots\rightarrow \\ \dfrac{13}{1} \quad \dfrac{12}{2} \quad \dfrac{11*}{3} \quad \dfrac{10}{4*} \quad \dfrac{9}{5} \quad \dfrac{8}{6} \quad \dfrac{7}{7} \quad \dfrac{6}{8} \quad \dfrac{5}{9} \quad \dfrac{4*}{10} \quad \dfrac{3}{11*} \quad \dfrac{2}{12} \quad \dfrac{1}{13} \\ \text{T.} \cdots\rightarrow\text{S.} \rightarrow\text{T.} \cdots\rightarrow\text{S.} \rightarrow\text{S.} \rightarrow \qquad \text{S.} \cdots\rightarrow\text{T.} \cdots\rightarrow\text{S.} \rightarrow\text{T.} \cdots\rightarrow\text{S.} \rightarrow\text{S.} \rightarrow \end{array}$$

D. C. 14:

$$\begin{array}{c} \text{S.} \rightarrow\text{S.} \rightarrow \qquad \text{S.} \rightarrow\text{T.} \cdots\rightarrow\text{S.} \rightarrow\text{T.} \cdots\rightarrow\text{S.} \rightarrow\text{S.} \rightarrow \qquad \text{S.} \rightarrow\text{T.} \cdots\rightarrow\text{S.} \cdots\rightarrow \\ \dfrac{14}{1} \quad \dfrac{13}{2} \quad \dfrac{12}{3} \quad \dfrac{11*}{4*} \quad \dfrac{10}{5} \quad \dfrac{9}{6} \quad \dfrac{8}{7} \quad \dfrac{7}{8} \quad \dfrac{6}{9} \quad \dfrac{5}{10} \quad \dfrac{4*}{11*} \quad \dfrac{3}{12} \quad \dfrac{2}{13} \quad \dfrac{1}{14} \\ \text{T.} \cdots\rightarrow\text{S.} \rightarrow \qquad \text{S.} \rightarrow\text{S.} \rightarrow\text{T.} \cdots\rightarrow\text{S.} \cdots\rightarrow\text{T.} \cdots\rightarrow\text{S.} \rightarrow \qquad \text{S.} \rightarrow\text{S.} \rightarrow\text{T.} \cdots\rightarrow \end{array}$$

*) S. $\longrightarrow$ can become T. $\cdots\rightarrow$ over a free bass.

27

┌──────┐ and └──────┘ refer to the 6 – 5 above and the 5 – 6 below the Cantus Firmus respectively, since these may be considered either as Ties or Suspensions. In the above table these are listed amongst the Suspensions because of their descending stepwise melodic motion, and not because of any implications of dissonance, although the latter may well be present in a multi-voiced texture.

8. When any of the seven basic inversions given in the above table are reduced by an octave so that minus intervals come about due to the inevitable crossing of parts a 4 becomes a –5, and a 5 becomes a –4, thereby changing the status of the interval from discord to concord and vice versa. For instance, in D. C. 9 the following intervals occur.

Ex. 15

But, when D. C. 9 is compressed into D. C. 2 these points in the inversion become

28

Ex. 16

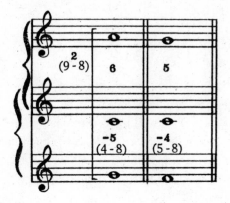

9. Before proceeding to the chapters that follow the student must study very carefully the Table of Inversions and experiment extensively with the dissonance resources of each D. C. inversion.

CHAPTER II

CANON IN TWO PARTS

1.   In order to qualify as a canon, a two-voice composition must meet three conditions:
   (1)   both voices will have the same melody;
   (2)   the melody will enter at different times;
   (3)   the entire mechanism will repeat without alteration, omission, or the addition of free material. Less rigidly constructed music must be relegated to the more general realm of Imitation. Of the three conditions stated above, only the last presents any problems in terms of Double Counterpoint.

2.   Before embarking upon the business of canon construction it will be helpful to establish a set of seven terms together with suitable abbreviations in order to simplify the identification and explanation of the processes involved:

   P   = Proposta, the voice that first announces the canon theme; the leader.
   R   = Risposta, the second voice to state the canon theme; the follower.
   c. u. = canonic unit, the note value in which the canon is calculated.
   u. v. = upper voice
   l. v. = lower voice
   m. v. = middle voice
   c   = interval of the canon
   m   = melodic interval
   v   = vertical interval

No other terms are necessary for the present.

3.   Before beginning a canon, the following aspects of the composition must be decided:

(1)   the initial notes of both P and R;

(2)   the time span (i. e., the number of c. u.) between the initial notes of P and R;

(3)   the time span (i. e. the number of c. u.) between the double bars which embrace the repetition of the canon mechanism. Thus, an elementary canon problem could be planned out and stated as follows:

Complete the following canon.

Ex. 17

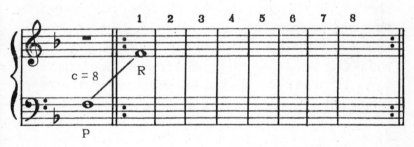

A technical description of the above problem would be: Canon at the 8ve at 1 c. u. lead in the P (the c. u. being the whole-note), with P in l. v. and 8 c. u. between the double bars.

4.   The canon can be completed systematically by means of a series of six steps carried out in the following order: *Step one:*   Copy in before the second double bar whatever comes in the P before the first double bar.

31

Ex. 18

This first step places the beginning of P (i. e., the portion that precedes the entrance of R) between the double bars so that condition (3) as stated in paragraph 1 above will come about automatically when the remaining four steps have been completed.

Step two: Block off twice as many c. u. before the second double bar as have been copied in in the P. (In this case 2 c. u. will be blocked off since 1 c. u. has been copied in.)

Ex. 19

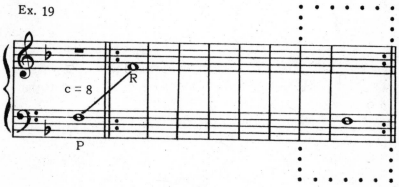

32

Step three: Continue P and R until the former comes up to the blocked-off portion, and the latter extends into it. (The following solution operates within the vertical and melodic limitations of 1st Species Counterpoint.)

Ex. 20

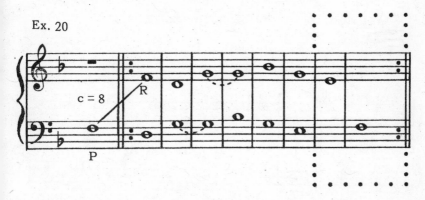

Step four: Tie over both P and R to a trial note "x", and add the interval between x and R to the interval between P and x to determine the D. C. inversion within which the repeat will operate.

Ex. 21

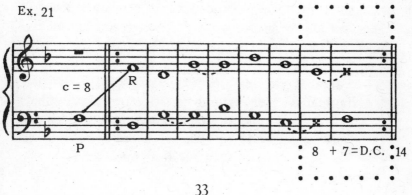

8 + 7 = D.C. 14

Step five: Referring to the D. C. inversion determined by the interval addition in *Step four* (in this case D. C. 14) in the Table of Inversions in paragraph 7 of Chapter I, select a suitable pair of intervals to substitute for those created by the trial notes (x) in Ex. 21 above, since these do not make correct 1st Species Counterpoint.

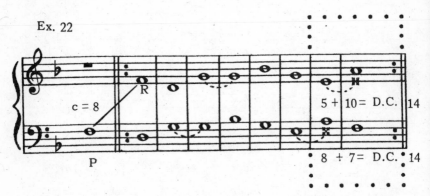

Ex. 22

It goes without saying that the sum of the trial note intervals and the sum of the intervals that are used to complete the canon must be the same. Now that the canon is completed the trial notes will serve no further purpose and may be erased. However, should the trial notes developed in *Step four* also produce acceptable counterpoint in whatever idiom is being employed, they may be used for the completion of the canon.

5.   For proof that condition (1) in paragraph 1 is fulfilled, the diagonal intervals throughout the entire canon should be checked. They *must* all agree. Should it so happen that the diagonal intervals are *not* all alike, somewhere an error has been made and the resulting structure is in that case not a canon.

34

Ex. 23

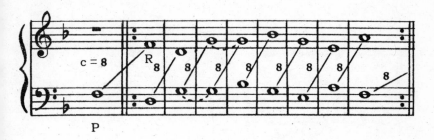

6.   The abstract canon as developed in paragraph 4 above can be used in all sorts of ways that are limited only by the composer's imagination and invention. The c. u. may be adjusted to any note value desired. And the canon may be embellished as the composer wishes. Ex. 24 shows two extremely simple treatments. In (b) the notes of the basic abstract canon occur at the beginning of each measure.

Ex. 24

35

The numerous techniques of canonic embellishment are treated in more depth and in far greater variety in a later chapter.

7.   The five step process demonstrated in paragraph 4 is the same regardless of the interval of the canon and whether P is in l. v. or u. v. The following problem of a canon at the 7th with P in u. v. and 10 c. u. between the double bars is carried out through the series of steps without comment or explanation.

36

Ex. 25

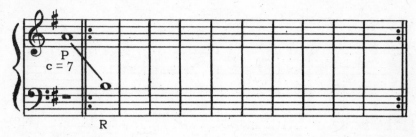

(a) Step one:

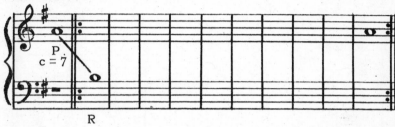

(b) Step two:

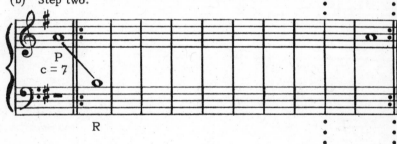

(c) Step three:

37

(d) Step four:

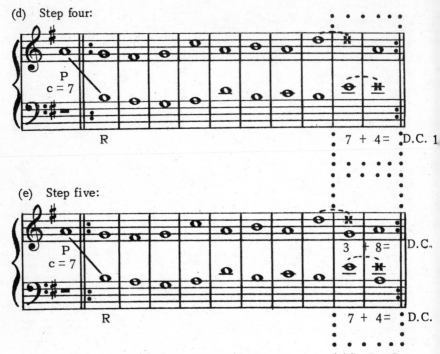

(e) Step five:

8. By means of the suspension resources within D. C. 10, the trial notes in this case could serve to complete the canon in the following manner. Ex. 26 is a reworking of *Step five*.

Ex. 26

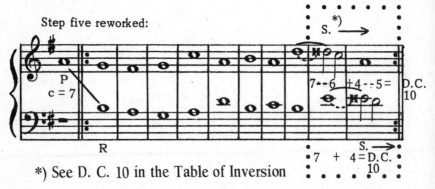

Step five reworked:

*) See D. C. 10 in the Table of Inversion

Many contrapuntal situations arise in which *Step five* becomes impossible within the 1st Species intervallic restrictions. When this occurs, correct dissonances provide the only solution.

9.   When two or more c. u. in the P precede the entrance of R, *Steps four* and *five* must be repeated for each one of these c. u. The problem to be completed is proposed in the usual format:

Ex. 27

Since there is no difference between this and the preceding one c. u. canons in carrying out *Steps one, two* and *three*, these are now shown simultaneously.

Ex. 27 continued

(a)   Steps one, two and three:

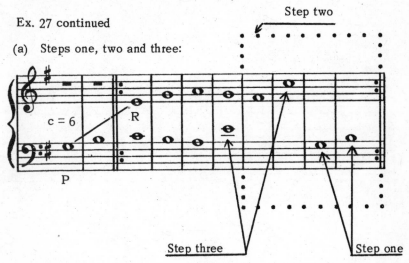

39

(b) Step four for 1st c. u.:

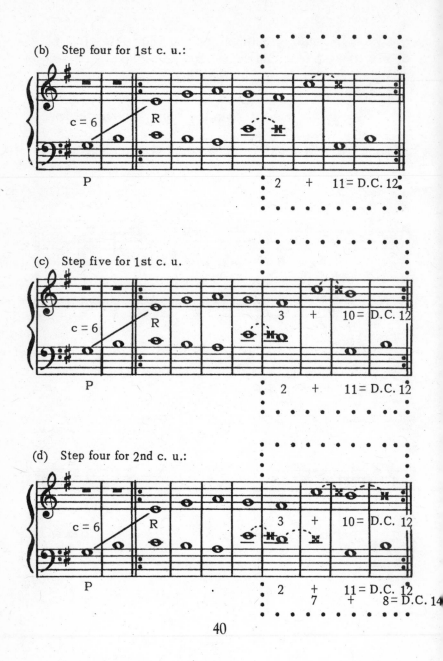

(c) Step five for 1st c. u.

(d) Step four for 2nd c. u.:

40

(e) Step five for 2nd c. u.:

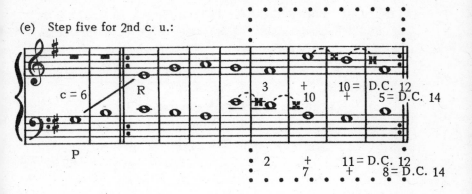

The canon is herewith completed, and can be used in any c. u. dimension and ornamented as elaborately as may be desired (cf. paragraph 6). The diagonal intervallic check for correctness will now be carried out as follows (cf. paragraph 5):

Ex. 28

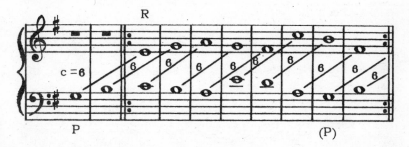

10.   The method demonstrated above makes certain the successful repeat of any two-part canon regardless of the number of c. u. involved, either before the entrance of the R or between the double bars.

41

11.   Only one additional observation is in order concerning two-part canons with two or more c. u. in the P before the entrance of the R. This has to do with the number of c. u. between the double bars, and has an effect chiefly upon the embellishing of the canon. The number of c. u. between the double bars may be

(1)   an even multiple of the number of c. u. in the P before the entrance of the R;

(2)   an odd multiple of the number of c. u. in the P before the entrance of the R, or less frequently,

(3)   no multiple of the number of c. u. in the P before the entrance of the R.

The canon developed in paragraph 9 is of the first type: 2 c. u. before the entrance of the R, and 8 c. u. (4 x 2) between the double bars. An odd multiple would place some number like 10 (5 x 2), 14 (7 x 2), etc. c. u. between the double bars. And, were the canon to be constructed so that no multiple of 2 would be embraced by the double bars, the number of c. u. would then have to be an odd number such as 7, 9, 11, etc.

12.   Aside from the embellishment problems that are apt to arise in the second and third types of time span between the double bars (measured in terms of c. u.) mentioned in paragraph 11, a more theoretical difference exists that may pass unnoticed in an analysis of the finished canon. Every canon wherein two or more c. u. precede the entrance of R actually embodies as many one c. u. canons as there are c. u. in the P before R enters. This can be shown by means of the completed canon in Ex. 28 by numbering the two given c. u. in the P before the entrance of R as (1) and (2) respectively and then indicating the two one c. u. canons originating therein by ———— and ··—··— as below.

42

Ex. 29

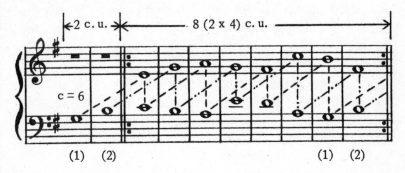

(1)   (2)   (1)   (2)

The above diagram shows that when (1) and (2) in P
return before the second double bar they come in the same
one c. u. canons as at the beginning. This would likewise
be the case if there were an odd multiple of 2 between the
double bars. But, were the number of c. u. between the
double bars not a multiple of 2, such as 9, the situation
before the second double bar would change since (1) would
come in the (2) one c. u. canon and (2) would come in the
(1) one c. u. canon. Ex. 30 shows how this operates when
the same problem is increased to 9 c. u. between the double
bars.

Ex. 30

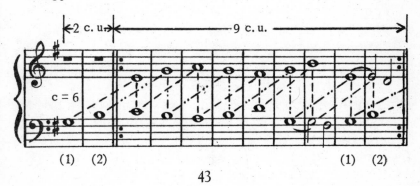

(1)   (2)   (1)   (2)

43

The same arithmetical principle of canon dimensions as discussed above is, of course, applicable to whatever number of c. u. there may be either before or between the double bars. Nothing further remains to be said about how a canon repeats.

13.   Before ending this chapter it may prove interesting to examine the construction of one canon in The Musical Offering by Bach. Somewhat enigmatic in appearance, it is presented thus:

Ex. 31

Bach

This is a canon at the 15th, P in u. v. with 4 c. u. (each c. u. being a ♩) in the P before the entrance of R and with 20 c. u. between the double bars. The obbligato between P and R is a free part and has no bearing on the mechanical structure of the canon. The canon together with the free part is given below in full with each c. u. numbered in both P and R. The free part is written in the treble clef so that it can be read easily at the piano if so desired.

44

Ex. 32

Shorn of embellishments and without the obbligato, the ♩ -note c. u. structure with its trial notes and double counter- point calculations appears thus:

45

Ex. 33

14.   As presented in the printed music the above canon has the double bars come after the first c. u. in the P. Once the canon is completed it is immaterial at what point the double bars are placed since the mechanism repeats automatically.

15.   From the principles set forth in this chapter it is possible to reconstruct for analysis purposes any existing two-part canon as well as to solve any repeat problem in an original two-part canon.

CHAPTER III

INVERTIBLE CANON IN TWO PARTS

1.   Just as Ex. 1 and Ex. 2 of the Introduction show an invertible two-part counterpoint and illustrate its intervallic construction, so can an invertible two-part canon be written. Such a mechanism, which yields two two-part canons, involves the simultaneous operation of three D. C. inversions:

    (1)   the interval in which the canon inverts,

    (2)   the inversion within which the upper two-part canon repeats, and

    (3)   the inversion within which the lower two-part canon repeats.

For an elementary problem: *compose a canon at the 6th, P in l. v. with 1 c. u. before the entrance of R and 8 c. u. between the double bars, invertible in D. C. 12, thereby producing a canon at the 7th with P in u. v.*

Ex. 34

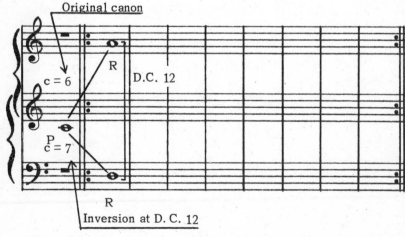

48

2. Ex. 35 shows the usual procedure, as established in paragraph 4 of Chapter II, carried through *Step four* in both canons at the same time.

Ex. 35

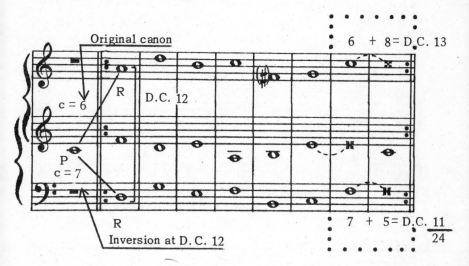

In every invertible canon the sum of the D. C. inversions within which the two canons repeat is equal to twice the interval in which the canon is inverted, in the present case $13 + 11 = 12 \times 2$.

3. While intervals within a D. C. inversion are added as shown in paragraph 3 of Chapter I, the D. C. inversions are added according to the usual arithmetic. The two kinds of addition that become an integral element of every invertible canon should not be too confusing once the process is understood.

49

4. *Step five* can now be carried out to complete the canons. But, before doing so, review the S.———➤, S.----➤, and T.----➤ resources within the three D. C. inversions involved, as given in the Table of Inversions in paragraph 7 of Chapter I. Ex. 36 shows *Step five* executed in both canons, that is above and below the P, without further explanation.

Ex. 36

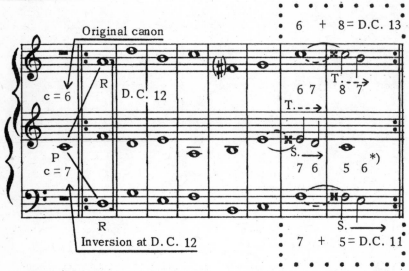

*) See footnote concerning ⌐_____⌐ to Table of Inversions in Chapter I.

5. When suitably embellished and performed separately as – perhaps – different sections of a larger composition, the two canons developed above within the Double Counterpoint technique might appear as shown below. Although the two canons are worked out simultaneously, the harmonic effect can be quite, and even surprisingly, unlike. This can be heard by comparing (a) and (b) of Ex. 37.

50

Ex. 37

6.   In a little vocal canon by Haydn the R together with its inversion (or more correctly, displacement) are used at once. The displacement is made in D. C. 3 (D. C. 10 – 8), so that the R is sung below P in parallel 3rds throughout the entire canon. (See Ex. 7 in paragraph 7 of the introduction.) Technically this can be described as a canon at the

3rd, P in u. v. with 2 c. u. (♪) before the entrance of R and 24 c. u. between the double bars; and with the R displaced in D. C. 3. As is the case in the Bach canon quoted in Ex. 31 in Chapter II, the double bars for use in performance are not placed where the double bars for calculating the repeat would normally appear. It is being left to the student to reconstruct the compositional processes and D. C. calculations through which this canon was evolved.

52

Ex. 38

Das größte Gut

Haydn

53

Upon the completion of the analytical reconstruction, it may be just a trifle disappointing to realize that Haydn seems to avoid any really challenging D. C. problems by means of repeated notes and rests.

7.   The above is *not* a three-part canon! It is a two-part canon with the R doubled through vertical displacement in D. C. 3.

CHAPTER IV

THE SPIRAL CANON—CANONIC RECURRENCE

1.   The so-called Spiral Canon is simply a form of the two-part canon as already discussed in Chapter II. The only difference is that in a Spiral Canon the repeat takes place at a pitch other than that at which the original entries of P and R occur. There are two general categories of the Spiral Canon: those in which the repeat is
   (1)   on another degree of the scale within the same key, and
   (2)   on the corresponding scale degree in another key.
The latter type is the more common. An example of each is shown below.

Ex. 39

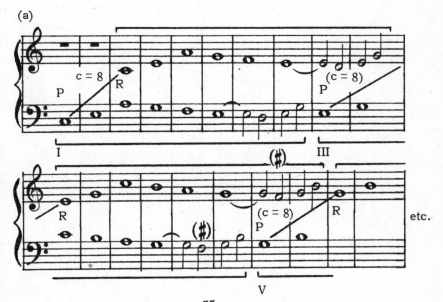

(a)

etc.

(b)

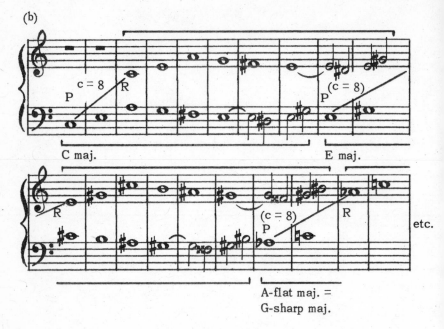

C maj.

E maj.

A-flat maj. =
G-sharp maj.

etc.

In (a) the repeat automatically occurs a 3rd higher for as many times as the canon is continued. In (b) the repeat will be each time in the key a major 3rd higher than the preceding one so long as the canon is carried on; in this case the series being C major, E major, G-sharp (enharmonically A-flat) major and C major one octave higher than at the beginning. Naturally, the proper accidentals must be inserted to modulate satisfactorily into each subsequent recurrence of P and R.

2.   Thus, by inserting different accidentals, the above canon could be adjusted to modulate upward by minor 3rds from C major through E-flat major, G-flat (enharmonically F-sharp) major, A major and back into C major one octave higher.

Ex. 40

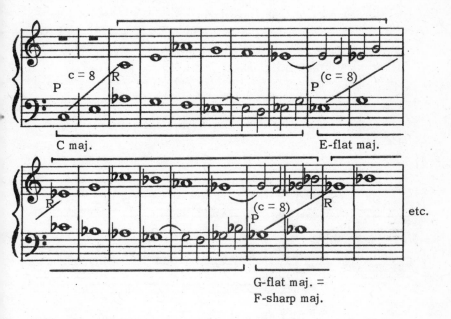

C maj.　　　　　　　　　　　　　　E-flat maj.

etc.

G-flat maj. =
F-sharp maj.

The illustrations in Ex. 39(b) and Ex. 40 happen to involve major keys. Minor keys are, of course, equally usable.
3.　Modulating canons (type (2) mentioned in paragraph 1 above) can spiral in any of the following intervals and return to the original key one octave higher or lower:

(1) minor 2nd, up or down　(4) major 3rd, up or down
(2) major 2nd, up or down　(5) augmented 4th, up or down
(3) minor 3rd, up or down　(6) 8ve, up or down

Spiralling by any other interval–the perfect 4th or any interval greater than the augmented 4th, except the 8ve–it is impossible to return to the original key within one octave above or below.

57

4.   When the canon is at some interval other than the octave or unison, the insertion of accidentals to effect a smooth modulation can present problems. In Ex. 41 a canon at the 5th, P in u. v. with 3 c. u. before the entrance of R, spirals downward by minor 2nds.

Ex. 41

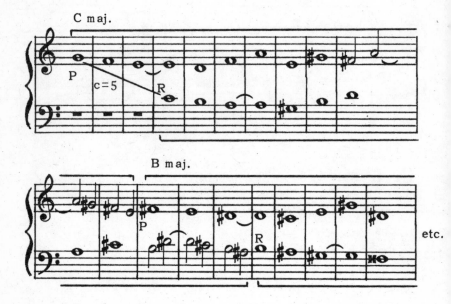

etc.

By reducing the c. u. from 𝅝 to 𝅗𝅥 and grouping them in three-beat measures, the above canon could appear for practical performance purposes thus:

Ex. 42

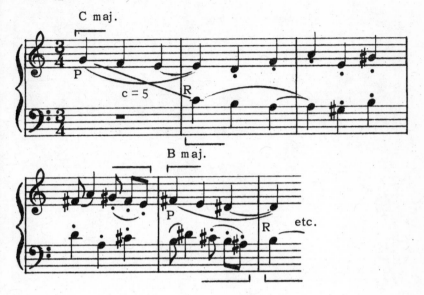

As a duet for two violins through the entire cycle of 12 keys, it would be expedient to begin an octave higher and end with a short coda thus:

Ex. 43

60

A-flat maj.

G maj.

F-sharp maj.

61

62

5. Except for *Step one*, the process for constructing the repeat of the spiral is the same as shown for the two-part canon in Chapter II. The illustrations that follow show the steps in the construction of the model in Ex. 39–40.

Step one: Copy in at the desired pitch and after the number of c. u. that are required for each section of the spiralling canon mechanism whatever c. u. appear in both the P and the R at the beginning of the canon.

Ex. 44

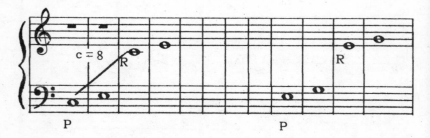

Step two: Block off twice as many c. u. as come in P before the return of R. (cf. Ex. 19 in Chapter II.)

Ex. 45

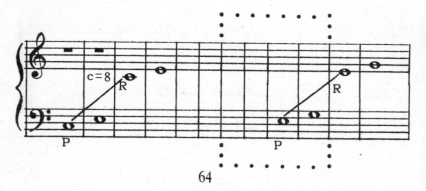

64

Steps three, four, and five:
Ex. 46

The accidentals can now be added, as in Ex. 39(b) and Ex. 40, and all subsequent repetitions will occur automatically however long the canon may be continued (cf. Ex. 41 – 43.).

6.   A Spiral Canon by Bach in The Musical Offering appears under the title "Canon a 2. per tonos" thus:

Ex. 47

Written out in full, the above canon together with the obbligato against which it is played appears as follows:

Ex. 48

Obbligato

R

etc.

P

67

The basic canon, stripped of its embellishments and divorced from its accompanying obbligato, is given with all of the D. C. calculations required for the repeat a major 2nd higher in Ex. 49. To say the least, it is proof of Bach's uncanny ability that he could embellish such an unlikely looking and intrinsically static canon into such beautiful and artistically successful music. His use of the rest eliminated one D. C. problem at the end. In a few instances the embellishing notes become both harmonically functional and ornamental, and are inserted in parenthesis.

Ex. 49

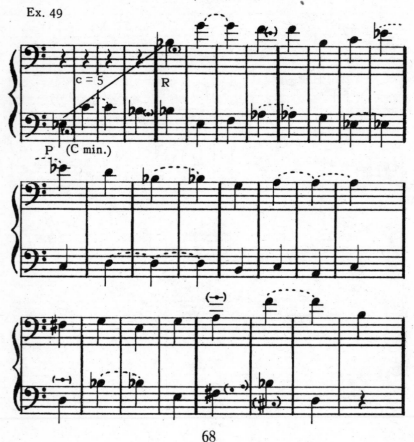

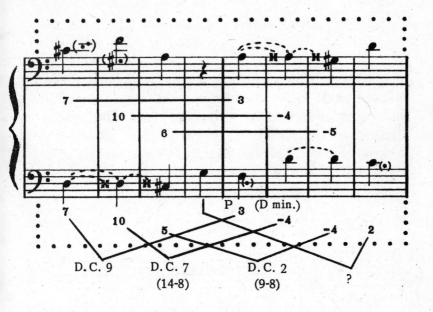

A confusing aspect of this canon in its original printed form is that the R cannot apply the accidentals literally since B-flat must be answered by F-natural and B-natural must be answered by F-sharp if the resulting harmony is to make sense. The entire key sequence is C minor, D minor, E minor, F-sharp minor, G-sharp minor, A-sharp minor (enharmonically B-flat minor) and back to C minor one octave higher than the beginning. The canon operates at the perfect 5th throughout.

THE CANONIC RECURRENCE

7.   The same technical process that makes possible the
Spiral Canon also enables a composer to bring in the
original canon theme at whatever pitch he may desire at
any pre-determined point within the form. One modest
illustration will suffice. A typical problem would be to
compose a canon with the original P theme brought in at
the specific points indicated:

Ex. 50

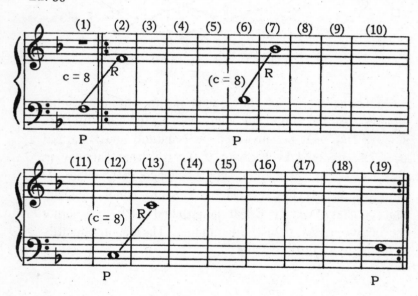

Steps *two, three, four and five* as required to bring in each
recurrence of the original theme, indicated by—.—.—, are
completed in Ex. 51 without further explanation. It will be

70

noted that the D. C. calculation process as employed here is exactly the same as that by which a Spiral Canon is solved.

Ex. 51

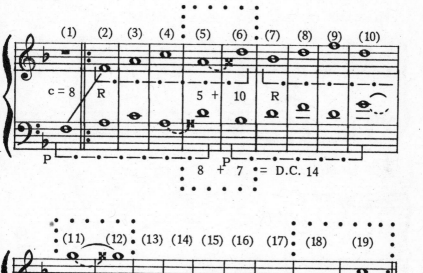

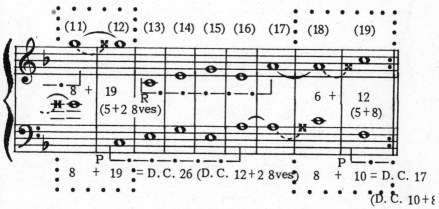

8.   The artistic possibilities of the Canonic Recurrence technique in a systematically planned and well executed form are limited only by the inventive skill and creative

imagination of the composer. A simple embellishment of the canon developed above may point the way to this kind of musical composition.

Ex. 52

Allegretto

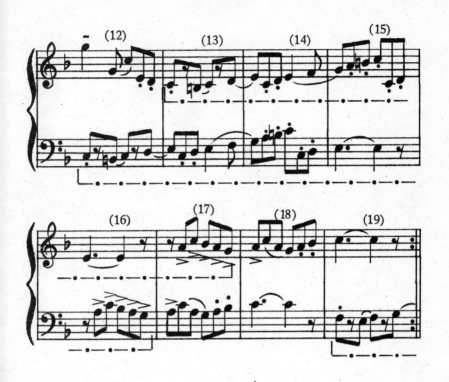

CHAPTER V

CANON IN CONTRARY MOTION

1.   A canon is in Contrary Motion when the P and R progress by the same melodic intervals, but in the opposite direction.

Ex. 53

*) In repeated notes no element of melodic direction in the present sense is involved.

2.   An elementary problem could be set up and stated as follows:

   Complete the following Canon in Contrary Motion.

Ex. 54

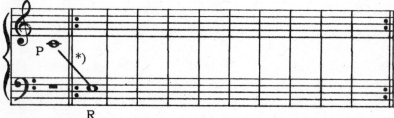

*) In a canon in contrary motion the "c" interval is not relevant in the same way that it has functioned in the preceding chapters, and will not be indicated in the present chapter.

3.   To effect a satisfactory repeat, proceed thus:
Step one: As in *step one* in paragraph 4 of Chapter II.
See Ex. 18.

Ex. 55

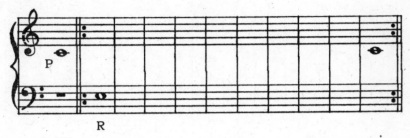

Step two: The same as *step two* in paragraph 4 of Chapter
II. See Ex. 19.

Ex. 56

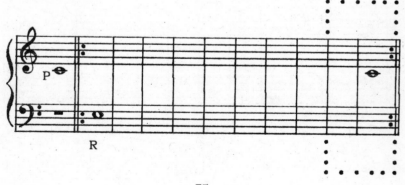

75

Step three: Continue P and R in contrary motion until the former comes up to the blocked-off portion, and the latter extends into it (cf. Ex. 20).

Ex. 57

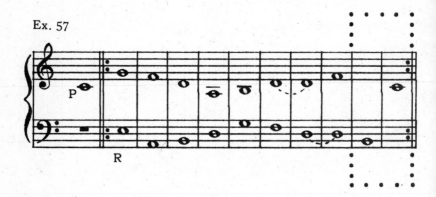

Step four: Tie over both P and R to a trial note x, and place in a vertical alignment the interval between x and R above the interval between P and x.

Ex. 58

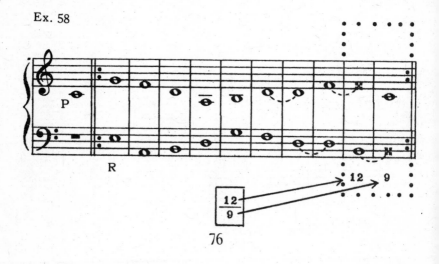

76

Extend this pair of intervals into a series *to the right by reducing* each number by 1 until the smaller figures reach 1, and *to the left by increasing* each number by 1 as far as may be desired.

$$\longleftarrow \text{ etc. } \quad \frac{14}{11} \quad \frac{13}{10} \quad \boxed{\frac{12}{9}} \quad \frac{11}{8} \quad \frac{10}{7} \quad \frac{9}{6} \quad \frac{8}{5} \quad \frac{7}{4} \quad \frac{6}{3} \quad \frac{5}{2} \quad \frac{4}{1}$$

N. B. Such a series of vertically aligned intervals does *not* represent double counterpoint, and has no relation to the Table of Inversions in Chapter I.

Step five: Select a suitable pair of intervals from the above series and complete the canon.

Ex. 59

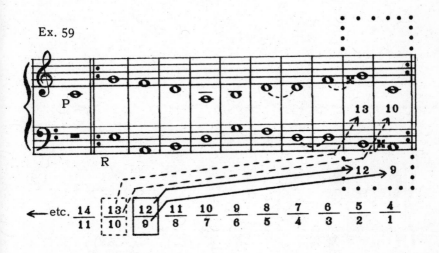

4.   When two or more c. u. in the P precede the entrance of R, the five step process as demonstrated above is carried out for each c. u. separately. Without further expla-

nation *steps four and five* are shown below in Ex. 60(a) and (b) as they were applied in the construction of the canon in Ex. 53 in paragraph 1.

Ex. 60

(a) Steps four and five for first c. u.:

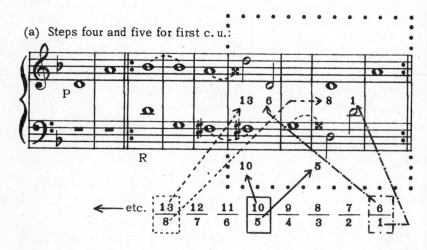

(b) Steps four and five for second c. u.:

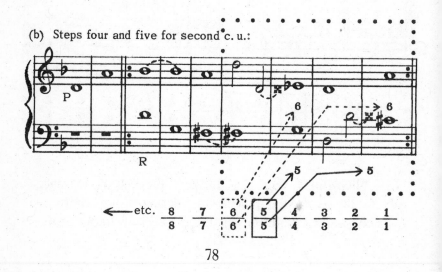

5. Under *Step four* in paragraph 3 the instructions say
that the pair of vertically aligned intervals resulting from
the trial notes (x) are to become part of a series that is
to be extended *"to the right by reducing* each number by 1
until the smaller figures reach 1." In most cases this is
quite sufficient. But, in a close canon it may become
necessary to continue the series beyond 1 into minus (–)
intervals. In Ex. 61 the trial notes (x) produce minus (–)
intervals so that the series must be extended right to give
additional minus intervals and left in order to arrive at 1.
The following shows only the canon as completed with
Step five.

Ex. 61

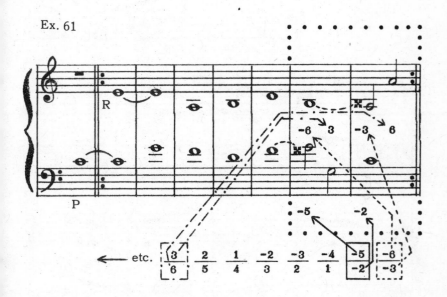

6.   Embellishments for a canon in contrary motion will, as is the canon itself, likewise be in contrary motion. This applies to chromaticized notes as well as to diatonic ones. Ex. 62 provides an extremely simple treatment of the canon in Ex. 59.

Ex. 62

It may be very difficult, if not outright impossible, to say with any degree of certainty what the duration of the original c. u. is once a canon is embellished. It could be argued quite convincingly that in the above canon the c. u. = ♪ , with 4 c. u. in the P before the entrance of R in the event that Ex. 59 were not in existence to support the fact that structurally the canon operates by 1 c. u. per measure.

7. A rather interesting canon in contrary motion by exact intervallic imitation appears in The Musical Offering by Bach under the caption, "CANON a 2. Quaerando invenietis.", with no point indicated for the entrance of R:

Ex. 63

Bach

8. The canon is calculated in the key of F major. It does not follow that it ''sounds'' in F major. Nor does it follow that it "looks" like F major. By aligning vertically the F major scale against itself in contrary motion, taking the 2nd degree of the scale as the originating point, it can be seen how the corresponding notes in P and R are derived. That is, the notes that are vertically aligned in the following diagram provide the corresponding notes that will occur diagonally in P and R in the canon. Chromaticized notes used in the canon have black noteheads.

81

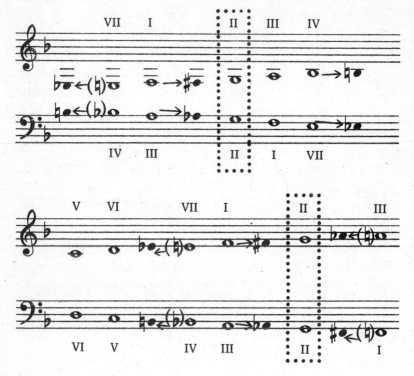

Written out in full, the canon will appear thus:

Ex. 65

The relationship of the above canon to the diagram in Ex. 64 will be seen at a glance when the R is placed directly below the P so that the corresponding notes are aligned vertically. The notes so aligned vertically will correspond without exception to those in Ex. 64.

Ex. 66

9. In order to reconstruct the repeat calculations a slightly different format will be helpful (cf. Ex. 31 – 33 in Chapter II). When the first double bar is placed immediately before the entrance of R in the usual way, it becomes clear that 10 c. u. come in the P before R enters, and 60 c. u. separate the double bars. The c. u. = ♩ , and all c. u. in P and R are numbered so that they may be readily matched with the diagram in Ex. 64. Ex. 67 shows the completed canon with *steps four and five* carried out for each of the 10 c. u. without further explanation or comment. Half-notes are rewritten as tied quarter-notes for c. u. identification.

Ex. 67

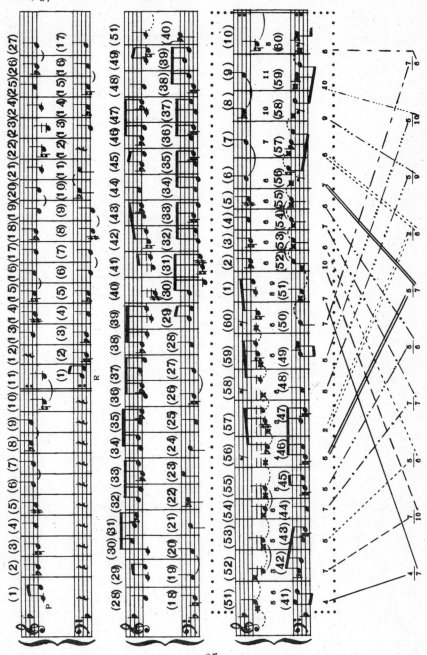

85

From the numerical information contained in the preceding diagram the reconstructing of the repeat through the 10 c. u. should present no problem. However, two of the series combinations may seem a bit confusing because of the embellishments until they are thought out completely:

$$\frac{(56)}{(46)} - \frac{(6)}{(56)} \quad \text{and} \quad \frac{(57)}{(47)} - \frac{(7)}{(57)}$$

10.   The Bach canon examined in Ex. 63–67 is in *exact* contrary motion *in one key with odd-numbered diagonal intervals*. On the other hand, the little canon developed in Ex. 54–59 is in *exact* contrary motion *in one key with even-numbered diagonal intervals,* operating diatonically in the key of C major. This possibility exists when the major scale is set against itself in contrary motion with the two lines originating on the fifth and sixth degrees of the scale respectively. Ex. 68 demonstrates how this situation comes about.

Ex. 68

When the P and R in Ex. 59 are aligned vertically as in Ex. 66 it will be seen at a glance how this principle works to generate the melodic lines.

11.   The chromaticized notes in Ex. 68 correspond to those suggested in Ex. 62, being simply an embellished version of the canon in Ex. 59. The student may wish to experiment with still more extensive and imaginative use of accidentals in this otherwise extremely simple canon.

12.   A canon in exact contrary motion can be constructed
with even more interest when the P and R are calculated
in two different keys. The final canon in The Musical
Offering by Bach, No. 6 captioned "Canon perpetuus,"
is so written. The P, assigned to the flute, is calculated
in D-flat major while the R, given to the violin, is structurally derived from the key of D major. The beginning of
the composition, which has a subjoined continuo part (not
included herewith), appears thus:

Ex. 69

By aligning vertically in contrary motion the scales of
D-flat and D with the intervening chromaticized notes,
beginning on the second degree of the scale (cf. Ex. 64),
and then aligning the P and R likewise (cf. Ex. 66), the
entire bi-tonal concept becomes apparent at once. Both
of these theoretical structural alignments are given with
no further comment in Ex. 70, but in the latter the chromaticized notes are indicated by "x." The music, despite
its bi-tonal origin, "sounds" in C minor with numerous and
varied transient modulatory effects.

Ex. 70

1) 8ve higher than in above diagram
2) 8ve lower than in above diagram

This closing movement of The Musical Offering is not, strictly speaking, a canon because the normal repeat process is not present. More correctly, it consists of two different canons so smoothly spliced together at measures 18 and 20, and again at the repeat, that it would take a keen listener to notice what actually takes place. The second canon reassigns the P and R themes and is calculated in the keys of A-flat and A major respectively. In the most rigid sense of the word, this movement can be thought of as a very skillfully wrought canonic fraud.

13.   Contrary motion canons can be developed in this way from any desired pair of major keys. Contrary motion canons in exact intervallic imitation cannot originate in minor keys, but can easily be made to "sound" in a minor key resulting from the fusion of two major keys.

14.   From the foregoing examples it will be observed
that canons in contrary motion fall into the following types:
      (1)   by inexact intervallic imitation,
      (2)   by exact intervallic imitation in one key
            (a) with odd-numbered diagonal intervals, and
            (b) with even-numbered diagonal intervals,
      (3)   by exact intervallic imitation in two keys
Type (1) is not illustrated in this chapter since it requires
no particular skill, and will occur quite naturally when the
originating point is taken at some scale degree (or degrees)
other than those shown in Ex. 64 and Ex. 68

INVERTIBLE CANON IN CONTRARY MOTION

15.   An invertible canon in contrary motion offers no
great difficulties in its numerical construction, but it can
present troublesome problems if it is to be written in
strict counterpoint. Since any such invertible mechanism
actually consists of two independent canons that must be
composed simultaneously, but performed separately (cf.
Ex. 36 and Ex. 37(a), (b), it becomes necessary therefore
to set up two intervallic series which will be applied in
opposite directions, one operating to the left and the other
to the right. Ex. 71 provides an example in D. C. 15
(D. C. 8 + 8), and consists of two one c. u. canons both
of which are in exact intervallic imitation in one key and
with even-numbered diagonal intervals. The intervallic
series operative in the two canons produce a crude ascending third-beat dissonance in the penultimate measure which
results in a rather successful suspension in the last
measure.

89

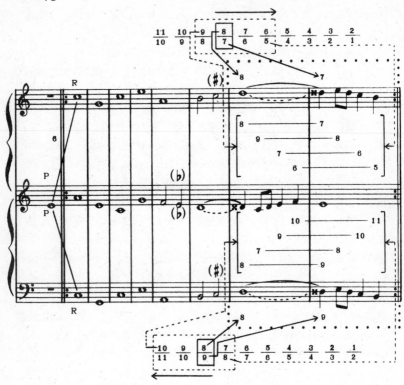

The above diagrammed method will suffice for constructing any invertible canon in contrary motion.

CHAPTER VI

THE CRAB CANON

1. A Crab Canon is one in which the theme operates against itself in retrograde:

Ex. 72

Such a contrapuntal device is also known as a Retrograde Canon and as Canon in Cancrizans Motion, the three terms being synonymous. When, as in Ex. 72 above, the canon theme is to be performed against itself at the same pitch, it can be written on one staff with the clef at the right-hand end of the line reversed.

Ex. 73

An 18-measure crab of this type is included in The Musical Offering by Bach as No. IV of "Canones diversi" under the misleading title of "Canon a 2." The student can write it out in full on two staves with no difficulty.

2.   In a crab canon the terms Proposta and Risposta are hardly applicable since the voices do not enter at different times. Nor is there any problem of a repeat. However, should a repeat be desired, a crab canon at the unison such as that shown above would not be effective because the two ends are in all probability the same. Thus, a strong repeat progression is conspicuously lacking. To repeat successfully, the theme in retrograde should be at another pitch to set up a satisfactory end to beginning progression.

Ex. 74

Here, in order to effect a satisfactory repeat progression, the theme in retrograde is one note lower than the original theme.

3. A crab canon is constructed within the D. C. inversion determined by the sum of its terminal intervals, which must be established before the process of any thematic invention is begun. In Ex. 75 the sum of the 8ves at either end is D. C. 15 (D. C. 8 + 8).

Ex. 75

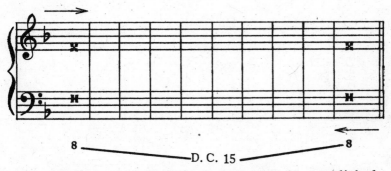

4. Once the terminal D. C. relationship is established, the canon will be composed inward from both ends until the thematic lines connect at the middle. Ex. 76(a) – (d) provide a note by note demonstration of this compositional working technique.

Ex. 76

(a) First progression from either end

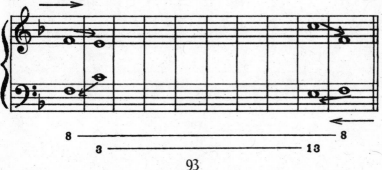

93

(b) Second progression from either end

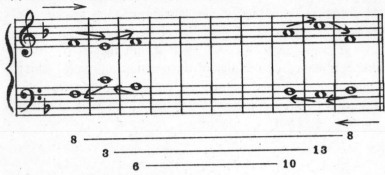

(c) Third progression from either end

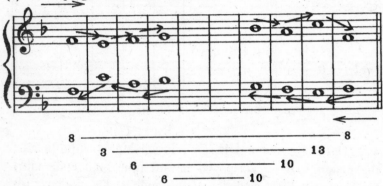

(d) Last progression from either end, bringing about connection at middle

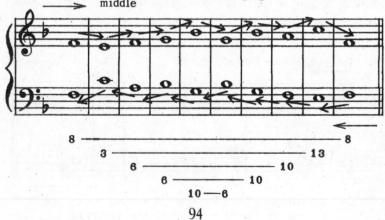

By means of the technique shown in detail above any crab canon, regardless of its length, thematic complexity or whatever its terminal intervals may be, can be written.
5.   A common structural feature with a resulting contrapuntal weakness exists in the crab canons in Ex. 72, in The Musical Offering, and in Ex. 76(d). All three are (1) derived intervallically from essentially the same D. C. inversion (Ex. 72 and the one by Bach from D. C. 1 (D. C. 8 − 8) and Ex. 76(d) from D. C. 15 (D. C. 8 + 8)), and (2) all three contain an even number of notes. The resulting weakness is a stagnant harmonic situation at the middle progression where the two halves of the canon are connected. These three ineffective middle progressions are as follows:

Ex. 77

(a) Ex. 72   (b) Bach   (c) Ex. 76 (d)

        −3   3   −3   3   10   6

95

This problem, which is inherent in D. C. 1 (D. C. 8 – 8) and D. C. 15 (D. C. 8 + 8), can be overcome by making the crab canon embrace an odd number of notes, thereby having as fulcrum one central interval instead of a progression. Ex. 78 gives two illustrations of such a solution: (a) consisting of 11 𝅝 derived from D. C. 1, and (b) 21 𝅘𝅥 derived from D. C. 15. Theoretically in each of these instances the central interval is a double interval inasmuch as it is approached from both directions. This, however, is purely theoretical and not audible.

Ex. 78

(a) 11 𝅝 derived from D. C. 1 (D. C. 8 - 8)

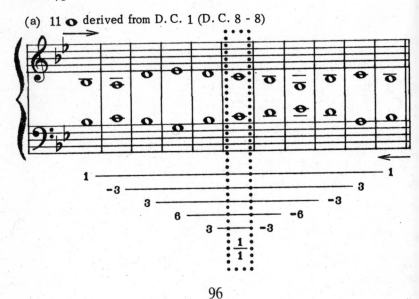

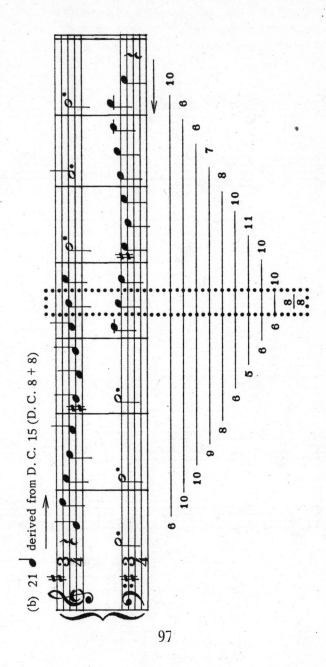

(b) 21 ♩ derived from D.C. 15 (D.C. 8 + 8)

97

It is impossible to derive a crab canon from D.C. 8 inasmuch as crabs can only be composed from odd-numbered inversions. 6. The problem of a middle progression does not enter into Ex. 74 since this crab is derived from D.C. 3 (D.C. 10 – 8)

Ex. 79

But, to derive a crab canon comprising an odd number of notes from D.C. 3 (D.C. 10 – 8) could cause contrapuntal problems at the middle because the central interval will unavoidably be a 2nd, the midpoint in the D.C. inversion.

Ex. 80

7.   From these observations it becomes evident that each D. C. inversion must be studied separately in order to determine accurately its middling possibilities for both even and odd numbers of notes. To this end the Table of Inversions is herewith given again but with one addition: the middle intervals of the odd-numbered inversions are boxed in with a solid line while in each of the even-numbered inversions the intervals that will become the middle when the inversion is decreased or expanded by an octave is boxed in by a dotted line. For instance $\dfrac{2}{9}$ in D. C. 10 becomes $\dfrac{2}{2}$ in D. C. 10 − 8, which is D. C. 3.

8.   An even-numbered D. C. inversion has no middle interval and, therefore, cannot serve in the construction of a crab canon. Thus, if it is desired to utilize the intervallic and melodic resources of D. C. 8, D. C. 10, D. C. 12 or D. C. 14 and the harmonic implications arising therefrom, these must be either reduced or expanded into the corresponding odd-numbered inversions of D. C. 1 or D. C. 15, D. C. 3 or D. C. 17, D. C. 5 or D. C. 19, D. C. 7 or D. C. 21 respectively (cf. Chapter I, paragraph 2). Up to this point D. C. 1, D. C. 15 and D. C. 3 have been illustrated in operation in the construction of crab canons.

9.   The Table of Inversions, with the additional indications explained in paragraph 7 above, follows without further comment:

D. C. 8:

	S. →	S. →	T. ⋯→	S. →				8. ⋯→	
8	7	6	5	4*	3	2	1
1	2	3	4*	5	6	7	8
	S. →	T. ⋯ →	S. →	S. →			8. ⋯→	

D. C. 9:

S. →	T. ⋯→	S. →	S. →	T.	S. →	T. ⋯→	8. ⋯→	
9	8	7	6	5	4*	3	2	1
1	2	3	4*	5	6	7	8	9
T. ⋯→	S. →	T. ⋯	S.	S.	T. ⋯→	8. ⋯→	T. ⋯→	

D. C. 10:

	S.		S. →	S. →		S. →		8. ⋯→	
10	9	8	7	6	5	4*	3	2	1
1	2	3	4*	5	6	7	8	9	10
	S. →		S. →	S. →		8. ⋯→		S. →	

D. C. 11:

S. →	T. ⋯→	S. →	T. ⋯→	S. →	S.	T. ⋯→	S. →	T. ⋯→	8. ⋯→	
11*	10	9	8	7	6	5	4*	3	2	1
1	2	3	4*	5	6	7	8	9	10	11*
T. ⋯→	S. →	T. ⋯→	S. →	S. →	T. →	8. ⋯→	T. ⋯→	S. →	T. ⋯→	

D. C. 12:

	S. →	S. →	S. →	T. ⋯→	S. →	S. →		S. →	S. →	8. ⋯→	
12	11*	10	9	8	7	6	5	4*	3	2	1
1	2	3	4*	5	6	7	8	9	10	11*	12
	S. →		S. →	S. →	T. ⋯→	8. ⋯→		S. →		S. →	

D. C. 13:

S. →	T. ⋯→	S. →	T. ⋯→	S. →		S. →	S. →	T. ⋯→	S. →	T. ⋯→	8. ⋯→	
13	12	11*	10	9	8	7	6	5	4*	3	2	1
1	2	3	4*	5	6	7	8	9	10	11*	12	13
T. ⋯→	S. →	T. ⋯→	S. →	S. →		8. ⋯→	T. ⋯→	S. →	T. ⋯→	S. →	S. →	

D. C. 14:

S. →	S. →		S. →	T. ⋯→	S. →	T. ⋯→	S. →	S. →		S. →	T. ⋯→	8. ⋯→	
14	13	12	11*	10	9	8	7	6	5	4*	3	2	1
1	2	3	4*	5	6	7	8	9	10	11*	12	13	14
T. ⋯→	S. →		S. →	S. →	T. ⋯→	8. ⋯→	T. ⋯→	S. →		S. →	S. →	T. ⋯→	

*) S. ──→ can become T. ⋯→ over a free bass.

100

10.   Embellishment, in the sense that it is demonstrated in the preceding chapters, cannot be applied to crab canons. Each note must be calculated separately. This is so because an interval that occurs on an accented note in the first half of the crab canon is inverted to an interval on a weak note in the latter half, and vice versa. Thus, in a D. C. inversion wherein a discord inverts to a discord, as in D. C. 15 or D. C. 17, an unaccented discord in the first half inverts to an accented discord in the latter half, and vice versa. Ex. 81 illustrates this rhythmic shift principle very simply in terms of D. C. 17 (D. C. 10 + 8).

Ex. 81

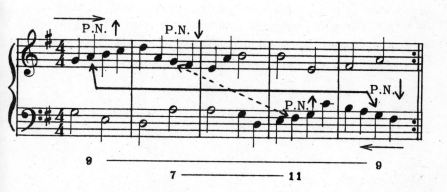

It is understood, of course, that a canon such as the above would not be used as a complete composition, but rather as a transitional section within a larger form.

11.   In triple rhythm the rhythmic shift of the inversion is as follows:

1st beat inverts to 3rd beat
2nd beat inverts to 2nd beat
3rd beat inverts to 1st beat

See Ex. 78(b) and Ex. 80 above.

12.   While this rhythmic shift of the inversion can cause contrapuntal problems in D. C. inversions wherein concords invert to concords and discords invert to discords, it becomes a help in those inversions where concords invert to discords, and vice versa. For instance, in D. C. 9, except for the central 5th which inverts to a 5th, all concords invert to discords, and vice versa. Thus, in a crab canon derived from this particular inversion, a discord that falls on an unaccented note in the first half will invert to a concord on the corresponding accented note in the latter half, and vice versa. An example follows.

103

A thorough study of the varied intervallic resources within each D. C. inversion in the Table of Inversions coupled with extensive experimentation will provide a complete working technique in the manipulation of the discords in every possible crab canon problem.

INVERTIBLE CRAB CANON

13. The composing of an invertible crab canon involves the manipulation of three D. C. inversions at once:

    (1) the D. C. inversion from which the upper crab canon is derived,
    (2) the D. C. inversion from which the lower crab canon is derived,
    (3) the D. C. inversion in which the crab canon is inverted.

The sum of (1) and (2) will invariably be equal to (3) multiplied by 2.

14. A specific problem could be stated as follows: compose a crab canon derived from D. C. 11 (condition (1) above) that is invertible in D. C. 10 (condition (3) above) to a crab canon derived from D. C. 9 (condition (2) above). Thus, $11 + 9 = 10 \times 2$:

Ex. 83

When working within such rigid intervallic restrictions it becomes virtually impossible to achieve acceptable counterpoint without (1) permitting some liberties and possibly crude dissonances, or (2) subjoining a free bass part.

105

CHAPTER VII

CRAB CANON IN CONTRARY MOTION

1.   The Crab Canon in Contrary Motion is the only canon mechanism that involves no structural application of a D. C. inversion. In contrast to the crab canon as discussed in Chapter VI, intervals in a crab canon in contrary motion are simply the same from either end. This is not to be confused with D. C. 1 as shown in Ex. 78(a) which utilizes minus (–) intervals. Ex. 84 illustrates how this curiously unsophisticated contrapuntally constructed device operates.

Ex. 84

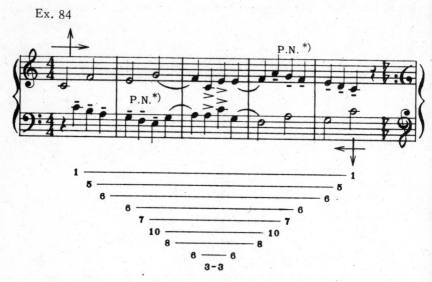

*) Although no D. C. inversion is involved, cf. Chapter VI, paragraph 10.

2.   The contrary motion crab canon shown above, by having had both voices begin and end on middle C, can be turned upside down and be read exactly the same as in its original position. Note the reversed and inverted clefs at the right-hand end of the music. It can also be written on one line in the alto clef thus:

Ex. 85

Such a presentation is possible because in the treble, bass, and alto clefs middle C comes on the middle line and therefore all C's relate identically whether viewed right side up or upside down.

Ex. 86

This is quite obviously more entertaining than pratical.
3.   When a crab canon in contrary motion embraces an even number of notes, the same interval (that is, numerically) is unavoidably repeated at the middle (cf. Ex. 84). This limits the melodic possibilities and harmonic implications of the canon because should the two adjacent inter-

107

vals that flank the middle happen to be unisons, 5ths, 8ves or discords, the result is an unfortunate contrapuntal progression. Thus, such a canon might be smoother in triple rhythm with an odd number of notes without any middle interval being repeated.

Ex. 87

This canon, not being in the key of C, can therefore not be inverted visually.

4. In a crab canon in contrary motion the problems of intervallic imitation are the same as those explained in paragraphs 8, 10, 12 - 14 of Chapter V.

5. A crab canon in contrary motion can be written in any desired D. C. inversion. The problem is simply to restrict the choice of vertical intervals to those which will invert successfully within the D. C. inversion selected. While all D. C. inversions are theoretically possible, a little experimentation will soon show that some of them are not too practical. Ex. 88 demonstrates such a canon inverted in D. C. 12.

Ex. 88

Every pair of vertically aligned intervals falls within the table of D. C. 12.

6.   More as a test of harmonic ingenuity than contrapuntal skill or inspired creativity, a four-part chorale style texture can be constructed by setting in motion at once two crab canons in contrary motion like that shown in Ex. 84 and Ex. 85; one in Bass and Soprano, and the other in Tenor and Alto. This method of construction accounts for the peculiar sequence of chords in Ex. 89.

Ex. 89

7.   The construction process for a harmonic texture such as in Ex. 89 can be seen by isolating the two constituent crab canons in contrary motion as in Ex. 90(a) and (b). Of course, considerably more freedom and motion can be

achieved by the use of more dissonant chords, greater liberties, accidentals, etc., but the basic structural problem and its solution remains the same. If it is not desired to make it visually invertible, a canonic texture such as the above can be written by the same process in any key and at any pitch.

Ex. 90

(a) Bass - Soprano

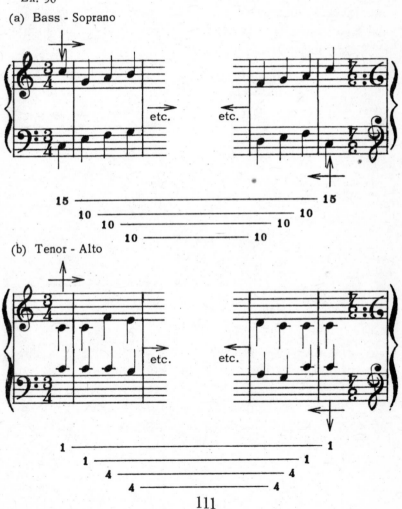

(b) Tenor - Alto

CHAPTER VIII

CANON IN THREE PARTS, I

1. A Canon in Three Parts consists of a Proposta and two Rispostas, hereinafter designated as P, R_1 and R_2. If one thinks of the three parts of the canon as soprano, alto and bass, there are six possible orders of entry in which P, R_1 and R_2 can function:

(1) S. R_1 ——————   (3) S. R_1 ——————
    A. P——————   A. R_2 ——
    B. R_2 ——   B. P——————

(2) S. R_2 ——   (4) S. P——————
    A. P——————   A. R_2 ——
    B. R_1 ——————   B. R_1 ——————

* * * * * * * *

(5) S. R_2 ——   (6) S. P——————
    A. R_1 ——————   A. R_1 ——————
    B. P——————   B. R_2 ——

The first four comprise type I and are discussed in the present chapter. The remaining two require a different technique and are treated in Chapter IX.

2. Picking at random entrance arrangement (2) from amongst the first four listed in paragraph 1, it might be worked out as follows:

112

Ex. 91

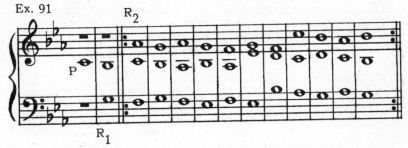

With simple embellishment this canon could be useful as a trio for three instruments, possibly two violins and cello:

Ex. 92

113

3.   The composing of a three-part canon brings into play two separate applications of double counterpoint to operate concurrently in the solution of the following two problems:

    (1)   the formation of the thematic line to generate a satisfactory sequence of harmonies in accordance with whatever harmonic idiom the composer chooses to write, and

    (2)   the achieving of an effective repeat.

These will be demonstrated separately as given above in the step by step process employed to construct the canon in Ex. 91.

114

4. The problem can be stated thus:
Complete the following three-part canon (cf. Chapter
II, paragraph 4):

Ex. 93

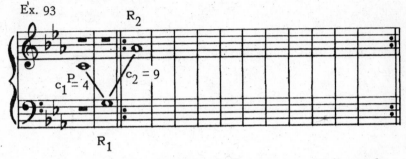

5. *Step one:* Let "C_1" and "C_2" designate the intervals
between the given notes of P and R_1 and of R_1 and R_2
respectively:

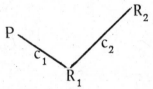

Then apply the formula

$$c_1 + c_2 = \text{D. C. inversion}$$

to determine the double counterpoint from which the canon
will derive its melodic contours and sequence of harmonies.

Ex. 94

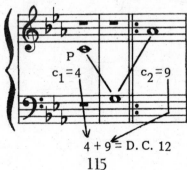

$$4 + 9 = \text{D. C. } 12$$

115

Thus, the structural interval of inversion is D. C. 12.

6. *Step two:* Proceed with the writing of the canon, and as each new note is added, let the vertical interval between P and R_1 be identified by "v_1" and that between R_1 and R_2 *in the subsequent c. u.* by "v_2". In every progression the following formula will be in evidence:

$$v_1 + v_2 = c_1 + c_2 = \text{D. C. inversion}$$

In notation the first progression in Ex. 91 will demonstrate the above formula as follows:

Ex. 95

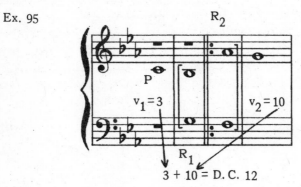

The second progression likewise:

Ex. 96

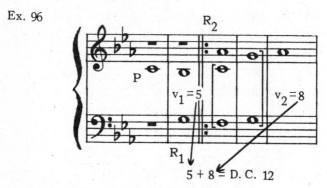

And so on throught the entire canon.

116

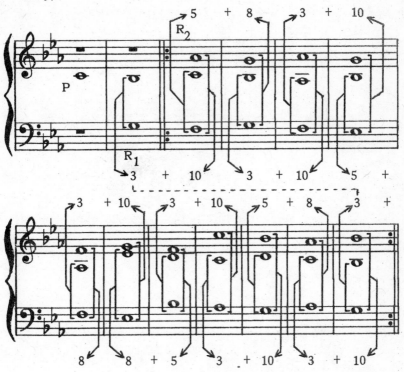

7. When more than one c. u. in the P precedes the entrance of R_1 and the same number of c. u. in R_1 precedes the entrance of R_2, the method of determining the D. C. inversion within which the canon will operate is the same as that shown in paragraph 5 above. Ex. 98 demonstrates *Step one* (cf. paragraph 5) in a three-part canon beginning according to entrance arrangement (1) as given in paragraph 1 above.

Ex. 98

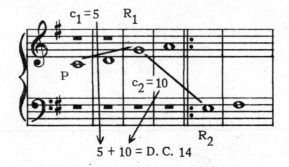

8. *Step two* applied to the first progression would appear as follows:

Ex. 99

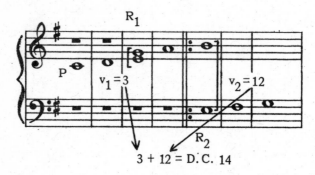

The second progression will be carried out in the same manner.

118

Ex. 100

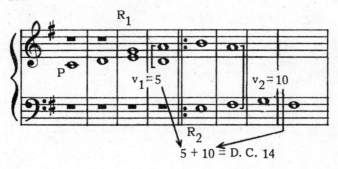

The process continues in this way until the end of the canon regardless of the number of c. u. in the P before the entrance of R_1. In order to show some of the more interesting features of a D. C. inversion such as D. C. 14, the canon is continued for a few more c. u.

Ex. 101

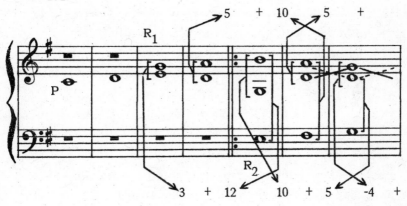

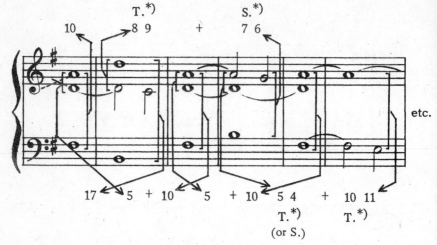

*) See D. C. 14 in the Table of Inversions.

It must be mentioned once again that this process of canon calculation in three-part canons is operative only when R_2 enters at the same number of c. u. after the beginning of R_1 as R_1 enters after the beginning of P. In other words, the entrances of P, R_1 and R_2 will be equally timed.

9. The repeat of a three-part canon presents a fairly complex problem. A three-part canon consists of three two-part canons:

$$(1) \quad P + R_1$$
$$(2) \quad R_1 + R_2$$
$$(3) \quad P + R_2$$

Each of these three constituent two-part canons will repeat according to the principles that are given in Chapter II. However, the repeat calculations must be made at a different time in each one of these two-part canons. It can be pointed out that of these three two-part canons (3) is the result of the D. C. calculations in (1) and (2), and is itself not directly calculated.

120

10.   The three-part canon developed in Ex. 97 together with the repeat calculations within the three constituent two-part canons is given in full and without further comment in Ex. 102 below. If the structural principles demonstrated in Chapter II have been mastered and the characteristics and limitations of each D. C. inversion in the Table of Inversions have been studied thoroughly, the problem of a repeat in a three-part canon should cause no great difficulties. With this background, Ex. 102 should be self-explanatory.

Ex. 102

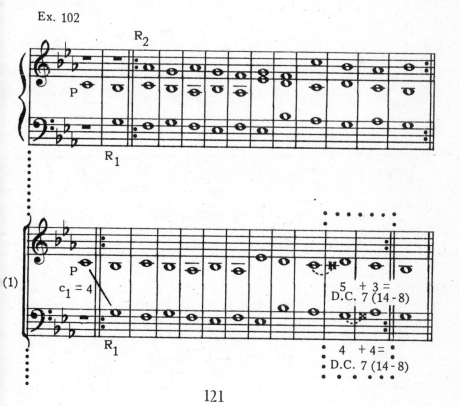

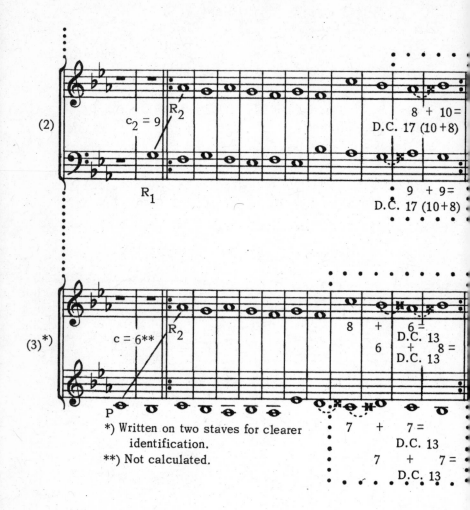

11. An extremely simple vocal canon by Haydn is presented in two of the entrance arrangements listed in paragraph 1. These are shown in Ex. 103 (a) and (b), and both versions are constructed within D. C. 15 with no dissonances involved.

Der Fuchs und der Adler

Haydn

(a) See Paragraph 1, (1)

Andante

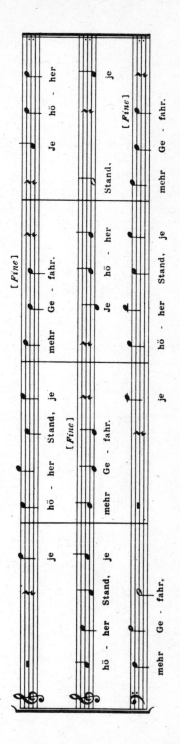

123

(b) See paragraph 1, (4)

Andante

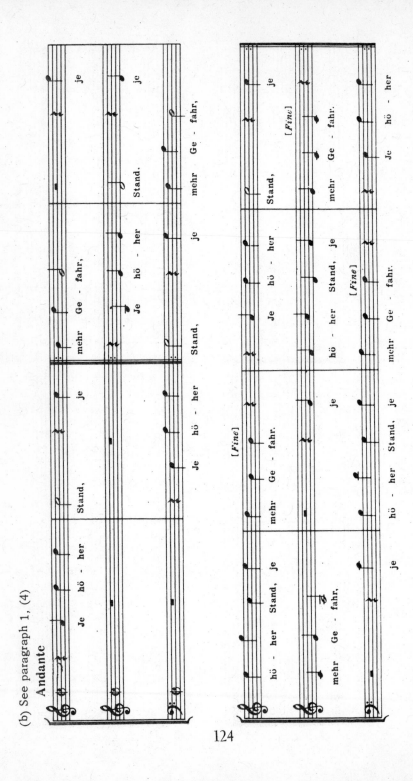

12.   In its basic unembellished form this canon can be seen as having each c. u. = $\d$, with the other notes of the harmony treated as embellishments in the 5th, 9th, 10th and 11th c. u. of each part. The entrances come 2 c. u. apart, and 12 c. u. comprise the entire canon theme. Ex. 104(a) and (b) show the structural aspects of the entire three-part canon as well as the mechanics of the repeat in full.

13.   In spite of the almost pretentious simplicity of this canon, one structural feature merits some explanation. Except for the unaccented note in the 5th c. u. of the P, no note produces a 4th or 5th against any other part. Thus, the canon is in the purest kind of triple counterpoint, which means that it can be performed in all six entrance arrangements listed in paragraph 1, since at no point will an objectionable six-four chord occur. The rule for writing a three-part canon in triple counterpoint can be stated thus:

When all three constituent two-part canons will invert correctly in D. C. 8 or D. C. 15, the total three-part structure will automatically be in triple counterpoint, thereby making all six vertical arrangements available.

The student would profit by experimenting with the remaining four inversions of this ingenious three-part canon by Haydn.

14.   Ex. 104(a) and (b) follow, and show without further comment the structural calculations in Ex. 103(a) and (b) respectively.

Ex. 104 (a)

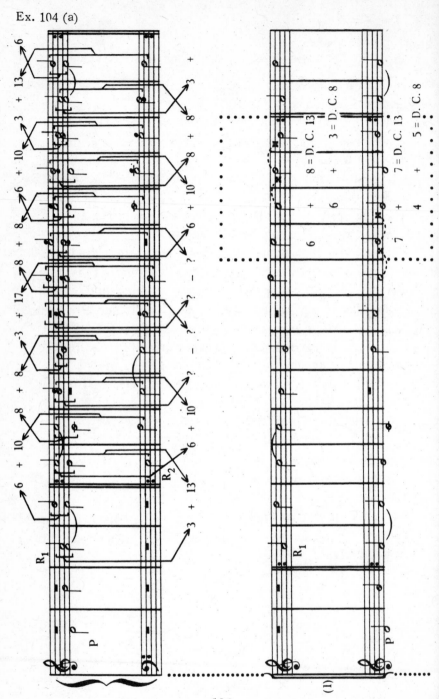

126

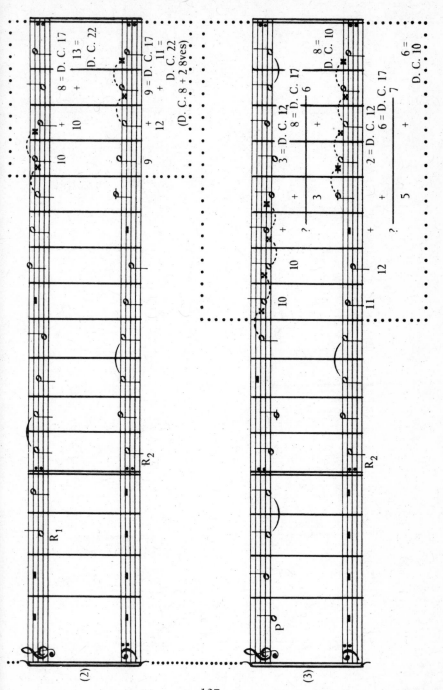

Ex. 104 (b)

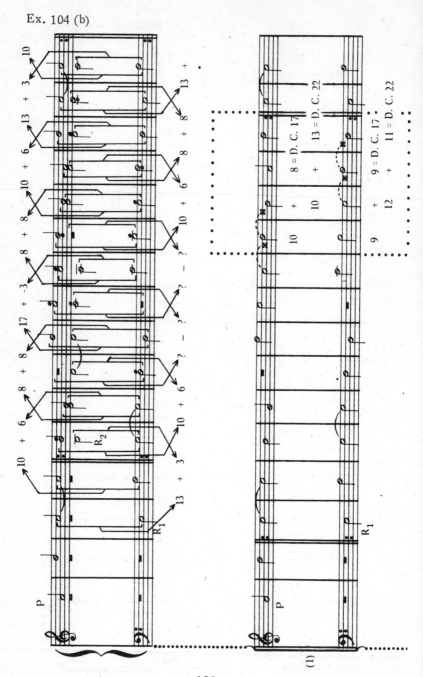

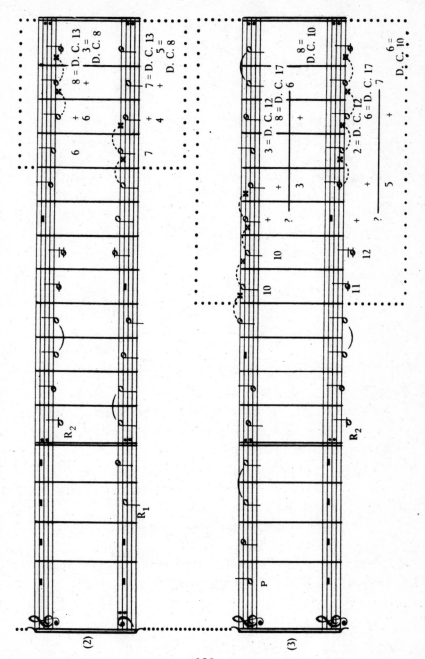

129

15.   The student can experiment in two ways with this canon for three voices by Haydn:

    (1)   try the remaining four entrance arrangements to determine whether they would work out successfully, and

    (2)   try to develop an embellished version of Ex. 104 (a) and (b) without the use of rests.

As to what may be uncovered by such experimentation, it will be observed that if the quarter rests at the beginning of R_2 and at the end of P were omitted, the progression at the repeat would be marred by some quite nasty consecutive octaves. It is not unusual for a faulty abstract canon to be improved by ingenious embellishment.

SPIRAL CANON IN THREE PARTS

16.   The technique demonstrated in Chapter IV for composing spiral canons in two parts can be extended to three parts. However, in three parts the contrapuntal problem can become at once vastly more interesting and correspondingly more difficult due to

    (1)   the possibility of involving restrictive D. C. inversions in the weaving of the harmonic texture of the canon, and

    (2)   the virtually unavoidable complexity in achieving a successful repeat.

A typical problem: *Complete the following three-part canon, derived from D. C. 13 to spiral upward by major 3rds.*

Ex. 105

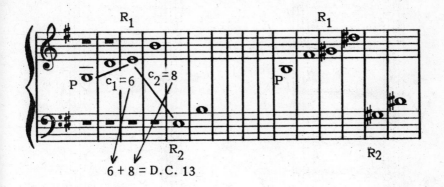

$6 + 8 = D.C. 13$

The complete solution follows.

Ex. 106

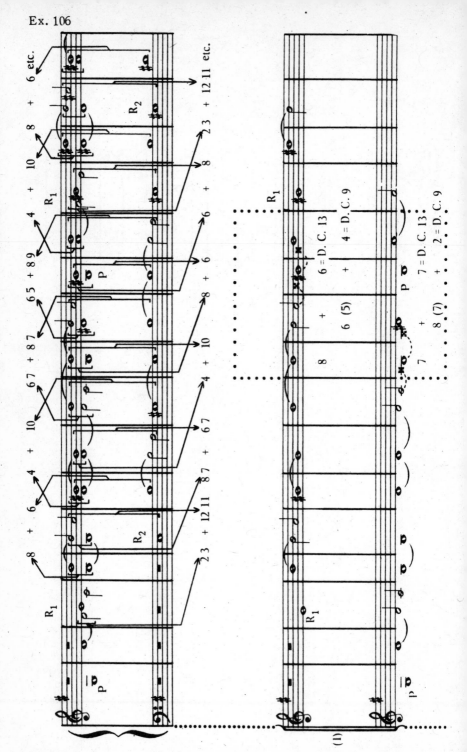

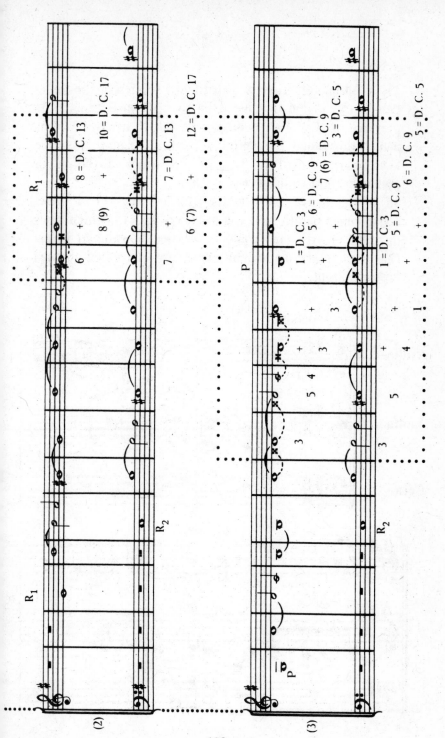

133

17.	An unpretentiously embellished version of the three-part spiral canon developed in Ex. 105 and Ex. 106 is provided in Ex. 107, scored very simply for two violins and cello. Since the spiral ascends by major 3rds, the key sequence will be G major, B major, E-flat major (enharmonic of D-sharp) and G major.

18.	The basic canon in Ex. 106 has one set of rather conspicuous parallel 8ves in measures 12–13, which show up more clearly than could be desired in two-part canon (2). It might be noted how these are concealed through embellishment.

Ex. 107

135

The above ascending canon can be continued throughout
the entire octave spiral as was done in the case of the
descending two-part spiral canon in Ex. 43.

19.   The Canonic Recurrence in three parts in constructed
by the same technique as is employed in writing the spiral
canon, and requires no further explanation (cf. Chapter
IV, paragraphs 7 – 8).

CHAPTER IX

CANON IN THREE PARTS, II

1. This chapter concerns three-part canons employing entrance arrangements (5) and (6) as listed in paragraph 1 of Chapter VIII:

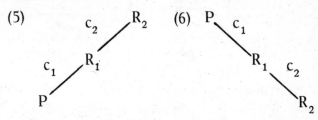

2. In these two entrance arrangements c_2 is not an addible interval and will be indicated within ( ), thus:

Ex. 108

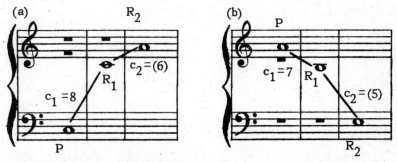

It is necessary to identify c_2 in this way because it is the 8ve inversion of the interval that must be added to that of c_1 in order to determine the D. C. inversion within which the canon is constructed. Ex. 109 demonstrates how this process of intervallic addition is carries out.

137

Ex. 109

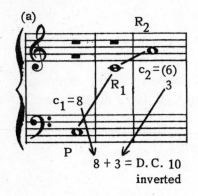

$8 + 3 = $ D. C. 10
inverted

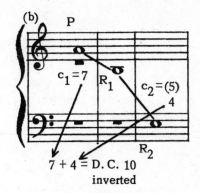

$7 + 4 = $ D. C. 10
inverted

3.   The inverted inversion principle can be seen at a glance when the D. C. 10 table is written out in full with the inverted inversions included both above and below. In each instance the number in ( ) is the interval of the inversion inverted in D. C. 8 (cf. Ex. 11 and the remainder of paragraph 2 in Chapter I).

	(-3)	(-2)	(1)	(2)	(3)	(4)	(5)	(6)	(7)	(8)
D. C. 10:	$\dfrac{10}{1}$	$\dfrac{9}{2}$	$\dfrac{8}{3}$	$\dfrac{7}{4}$	$\dfrac{6}{5}$	$\dfrac{5}{6}$	$\dfrac{4}{7}$	$\dfrac{3}{8}$	$\dfrac{2}{9}$	$\dfrac{1}{10}$
inverted										
	(8)	(7)	(6)	(5)	(4)	(3)	(2)	(1)	(-2)	(-3)

Ex. 109 (a)   Ex. 109 (b)

4.   In like manner, v_2 is not addible and must be treated in the same way as c_2 is treated. Ex. 110(a) and (b) demonstrate the $v_1 + v_2$ addition for a few c. u. in the canons set up by the beginnings in Ex. 109(a) and (b).

Ex. 110

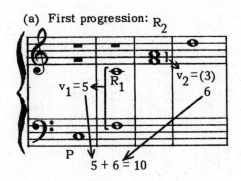

(a) First progression: R₂

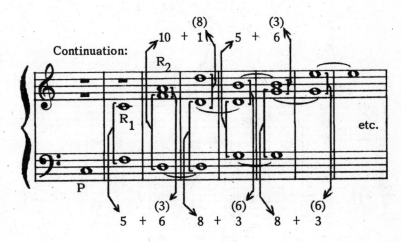

Continuation:

139

(b) First progression:

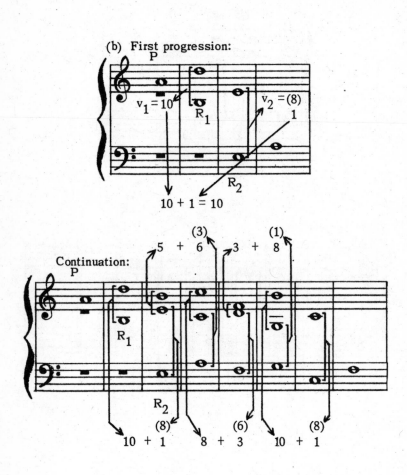

5. When the P moves away from R_1 to produce a v_1 greater than the structural D. C. inversion currently in force,

Ex. 111

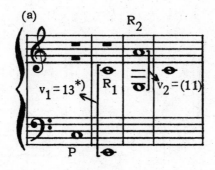

(a)

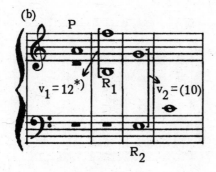

(b)

*) Greater than the interval of inversion, D. C. 10

141

then, in order to achieve the proper D. C. addition sub-
tract 8 from both v_1 and v_2 before making the intervallic
calculations. This is demonstrated in Ex. 112.

Ex. 112

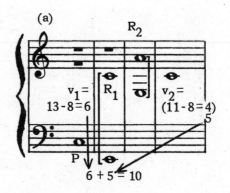

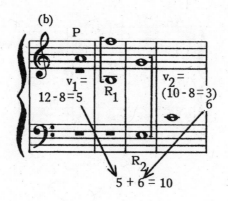

6.   Whenever v_1 and v_2 are equal, the structural inverted interval of inversion is always D. C. 8.

7.   Concerning repeats, there is nothing to add to what is shown in Chapter VIII, beginning at paragraph 9.

8.   The student is urged to experiment with those D. C. inversions wherein most of the concords invert to discords, and vice versa. As a typical problem of this type, Ex. 113 shows a three-part canon in entrance arrangement (5), with 3 c. u. separating the entrance of P – R_1 and R_1 – R_2 respectively, being constructed within the inverted inversion of D. C. 14:

$$
\text{D. C. 14:} \quad
\begin{array}{ccccccc}
(-7) & (-6) & (-5) & (-4) & (-3) & (-2) & (1) \\
14 & 13 & 12 & 11 & 10 & 9 & 8 \\
\hline
1 & 2 & 3 & 4 & 5 & 6 & 7 \\
(8) & (7) & (6) & (5) & (4) & (3) & (2)
\end{array}
$$

$$
\begin{array}{ccccccc}
(2) & (3) & (4) & (5) & (6) & (7) & (8) \\
7 & 6 & 5 & 4 & 3 & 2 & 1 \\
\hline
8 & 9 & 10 & 11 & 12 & 13 & 14 \\
(1) & (-2) & (-3) & (-4) & (-5) & (-6) & (-7)
\end{array}
$$

The problem: *Complete the following three-part canon:*

Ex. 113

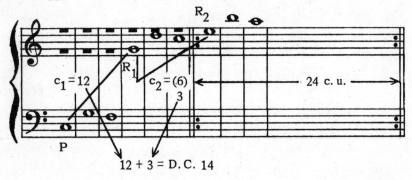

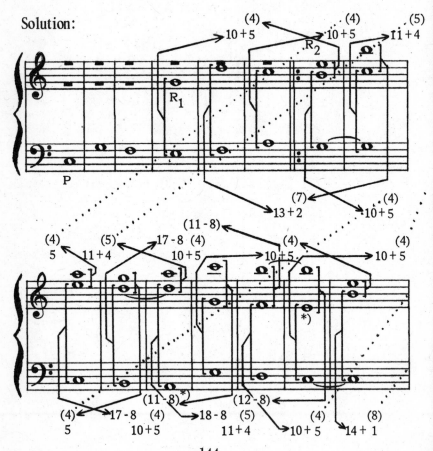

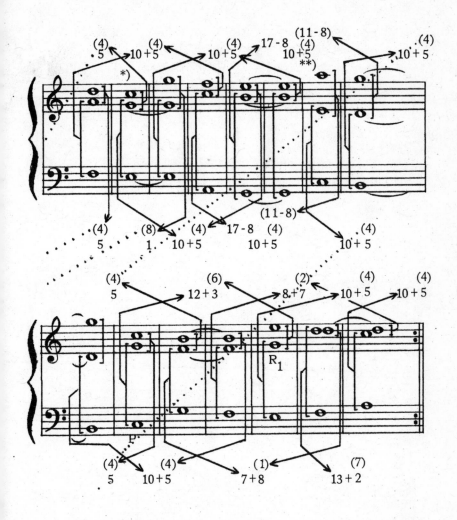

*) This c. u. omitted in embellished version in Ex. 114.
   See rests on the 2nd beat in measure 2, 3, and 4 after
   the first double bar.
**) Repeated.

145

The repeat calculations within the three constituent two-part canons can be readily analyzed on the basis of what is shown in this regard in Chapter VIII. No further explanation of this process is required here. A slightly embellished version of the above three-part canon with each c. u.

reduced to a ♩ , and scored for string trio is given in Ex. 114. A short coda is appended so that the canon can be brought to a practical ending when performed.

Ex. 114

Coda (free material)

*) Cf. footnote *) to Ex. 113.

CHAPTER X

CANON IN FOUR AND MORE PARTS
CANON WITH UNEQUALLY SPACED ENTRANCES

1. A canon in more than three voices embodies a fixed number of constituent canons of three different types:

    (1)   calculated three-part canons (with equally spaced entrances),

    (2)   uncalculated three-part canons (some with unequally and some with equally spaced entrances),

    (3)   two-part canons.

For instance, a four-part canon, consisting of P, R_1, R_2, R_3

Ex. 115

contains within itself

    (1) 2 interlocking calculated three-part canons:

$P - R_1 - R_2$ ──────

$R_1 - R_2 - R_3$ ············

148

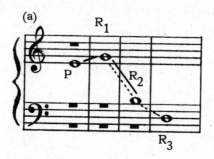

(2) 2 interlocking uncalculated three-part canons:

$$P - R_1 - R_3 \quad \text{-------}$$

$$P - R_2 - R_3 \quad \text{-·--·--·--·}$$

Ex. 115

(3) 6 two-part canons:

$$P - R_1 \qquad\qquad R_1 - R_2$$
$$P - R_2 \qquad\qquad R_1 - R_3$$
$$P - R_3 \qquad\qquad R_2 - R_3$$

It is at once evident that with so many constituent canons in operation at once, a four-part canon is a highly complex contrapuntal mechanism.

2. The structural components of multi-voiced canons can be tabulated as follows:

	Calculated 3–part Canons	Uncalculated 3–part Canons	2–part Canons
4–part Canon:	2	2	6
5–part Canon:	3	7	10
6–part Canon:	4	16	15
7–part Canon:	5	30	21
8–part Canon:	6	50	28

A little experimentation will readily show how this arithmetical situation comes about. More than 8 parts, while theoretically possible, is hardly practical either structurally or musically.

3. In paragraph 1 of Chapter VIII it is shown how a canon in three parts can have 6 possible entrance arrangements of P, R_1 and R_2. As the number of parts, that is the number of Rispostas, is increased the number of possible entrance arrangements is correspondingly increased according to the following table:

4–part Canon:	24 entrance arrangements are possible
5–part Canon:	120 entrance arrangements are possible
6–part Canon:	720 entrance arrangements are possible
7–part Canon:	5040 entrance arrangements are possible
8–part Canon:	40320 entrance arrangements are possible

However, regardless of the number of parts in the canon, the constituent three-part canons will fall within the six entrance arrangements listed in paragraph 1 of Chapter

VIII. In the four-part beginning used for illustration purposes in Ex. 115, the interlocking three-part canons are
of types (1) and (6) respectively (cf. Chapter VIII, paragraph 1), and must be calculated accordingly.

Ex. 116

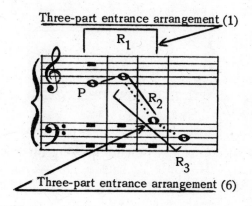

Thus, the formation of the two calculated three-part canons
in the above beginning can be treated as follows:

Ex. 116

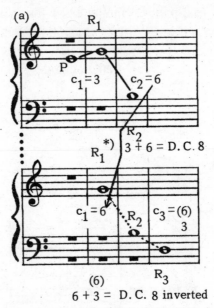

*) In the second of the two interlocking three-part canons R_1 serves as P, while R_2 and R_3 serve as R_1 and R_2 respectively.

The two calculated three-part canons will then operate in the two inversions as demonstrated below. It will be observed that c_2 of the first three-part canon becomes c_1 of the second. The complete calculation process proceeds as shown by the arrows.

$$\text{D. C. 8:} \quad \frac{8}{1} \quad \frac{7}{2} \quad \frac{6}{3} \quad \frac{5}{4} \quad \frac{4}{5} \quad \frac{3}{6} \quad \frac{2}{7} \quad \frac{1}{8}$$

$$\begin{array}{ccccccccc}
& (1) & (2) & (3) & (4) & (5) & (6) & (7) & (8) \\
\text{D. C. 8} & \dfrac{8}{1} & \dfrac{7}{2} & \dfrac{6}{3} & \dfrac{5}{4} & \dfrac{4}{5} & \dfrac{3}{6} & \dfrac{2}{7} & \dfrac{1}{8} \\
\text{inverted:} & (8) & (7) & (6) & (5) & (4) & (3) & (2) & (1)
\end{array}$$

4. Within the two calculated three-part canons v_1 and v_2 follow the same D. C. process as c_1 and c_2. By this method, the first progression of the four-part canon currently under construction can be carried out as follows:

Ex. 117

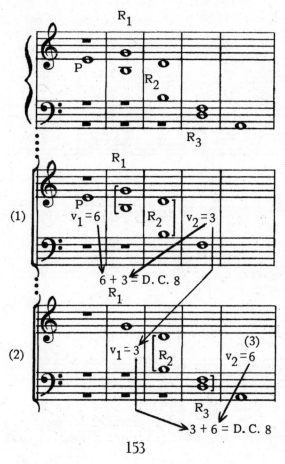

153

D. C. 8: $\dfrac{8}{1}$ $\dfrac{7}{2}$ $\left(\dfrac{6}{3}\right.$ $\dfrac{5}{4}$ $\dfrac{4}{5}$ $\dfrac{3}{6}$ $\dfrac{2}{7}$ $\dfrac{1}{8}$

	(1)	(2)	(3)	(4)	(5)	(6)	(7)	(8)
D. C. 8 inverted:	$\dfrac{8}{1}$	$\dfrac{7}{2}$	$\dfrac{6}{3}$	$\dfrac{5}{4}$	$\dfrac{4}{5}$	$\dfrac{3}{6}$	$\dfrac{2}{7}$	$\dfrac{1}{8}$
	(8)	(7)	(6)	(5)	(4)	(3)	(2)	(1)

Within the same format and without further comment, the complete canon is given in Ex. 118. For purposes of expediency—to keep awkward voice-leading and doublings to a minimum—the canon is tonaliticized in B-flat major.

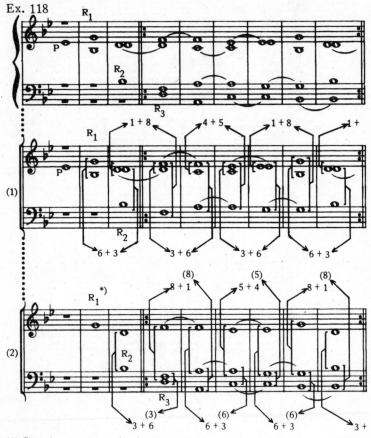

Ex. 118

*) See footnote to Ex. 116(a).

5. Within the four three-part canons embodied within the one four-part canon (two calculated and two uncalculated), six two-part canons are also in operation (cf. paragraph 1 and 2 above). It is upon these, basically, that the repeat depends. These six two-part canons as they are contained in Ex. 118 can be demonstrated as follows:

Ex. 119

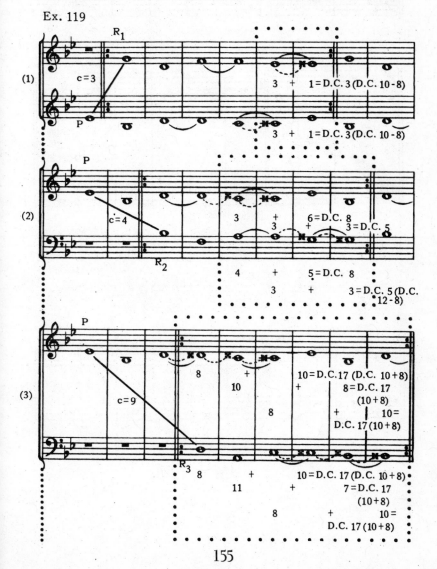

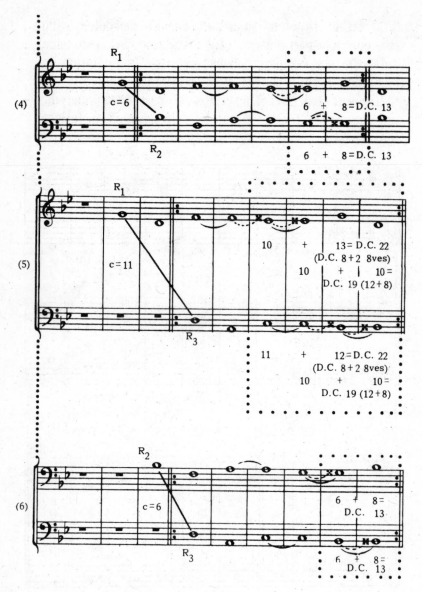

156

6.   The four-part canon developed in Ex. 115 – 119 is relatively unsophisticated mechanically due to the fact that both of the calculated component three-part canons are derived from D. C. 8. For this reason the great majority of the multi-voiced canons in the musical literature are so constructed. The problem becomes considerably more involved when the calculated three-part canons represent different intervals of inversion. Such a case is the canon problem proposed in Ex. 120. Here the mechanism operates within D. C. 12 and the inverted inversion of D. C. 10 respectively.

Ex. 120

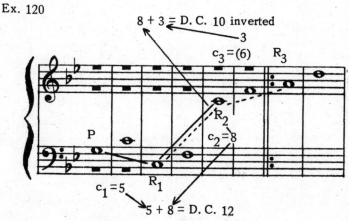

A possible solution to the above problem within the most conservative textural resources follows in Ex. 121 with the two constituent three-part canons in score. Greater· linear flexibility could be achieved by permitting more freedom in the introduction and resolution of discords. Such freedom, however, is brought about by the artistic requirements of the composer and does not affect the arithmetical calculation of the canon. Ex. 121 is given with all calculations in the usual manner, but without further explanation.

157

Ex. 121

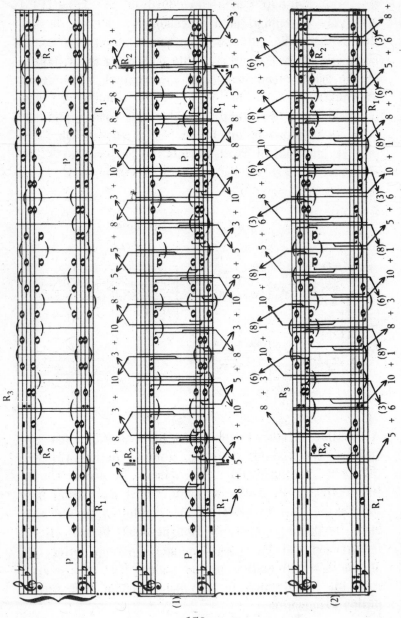

158

The two-part canons and their repeat calculations can be written out as in Ex. 119 if so desired.

7.   As the D. C. calculations within a multi-voiced canon are made more complex, the embellishment problem assumes new dimensions. Outwardly, this becomes evident in three specific respects:

(1)   fewer melodic possibilities exist that do not create inept contrapuntal situations, such as parallel fifths or octaves;

(2)   added liberties in the use of dissonances become inevitable, and

(3)   the melodic lines, though relatively unadorned, generate a peculiar kind of "drive".

Ex. 122 is a modest and conservatively embellished version of the above four-part canon in score for string quartet. One may profit from experimenting in seeking to achieve greater melodic flexibility without resorting to unacceptable contrapuntal compromises.

Ex. 122

160

161

A coda or epilogue in any desired proportion to the canon can be added to bring the composition to an artistically satisfactory close as regards time, tonality, and harmony.

THE THREE-PART CANON IN VERTICAL ALIGNMENT

8.   In order accurately to determine in advance the melodic possibilities of any multi-voiced canon it is merely necessary to see all of the constituent three-part canons in their respective vertical alignments. By this method one can tell at a glance what melodic intervals are available within the harmonic idiom desired.

9.   The vertical alignment of entrance arrangements (1)–(4) listed in paragraph 1 of Chapter VIII as carried out in the following series of steps:

Step one: Determine the structural D. C. inversion by adding c_1 and c_2 in the usual way.

Ex. 123

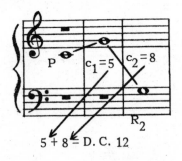

Step two: On a three-stave system as used for double counterpoint place the initial note of P on the middle line.

Ex. 124

Step three: In the subsequent c. u., on the staff either above or below as the case may be, place the initial note of R_1 exactly as it comes in the given canon beginning.

Ex. 125

163

Step four: On the remaining staff, either lowest or uppermost as the case may be, write a note at the interval below or above R_1 that is determined by adding c_1 and c_2 (cf. *Step one* above).

Ex. 126

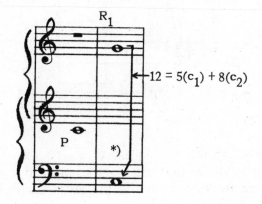

*) Except when c_1 and c_2 are both 8 (or 1 or 15) this will *not* be the initial note of R_2.

Step five: Let P proceed by a melodic interval (m) to form suitable intervals for v_1 and v_2 within the structural D. C. inversion, thus:

Ex. 127

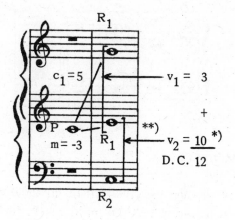

*) This is the interval, but *not* the notes, of v_2
**) In this vertical alignment the note on the middle staff for purposes of calculation serves a double function: as P in v_1 and as R_1 in v_2.

10.   A pair of concurrently functioning formulae hereby comes into operation thus:

$$(1) \quad c_1 \pm m = v_1$$
$$(2) \quad D.\,C. - v_1 = v_2$$

The melodic interval, m, is minus (–) when P moves *towards* R_1, and plus (+) when P moves *away from* R_1. In the canon progression the above vertical alignment is applied thus:

165

Ex. 128

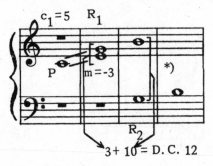

*) See footnote *) to Ex. 127

By means of the above method all of the melodic intervals (m) and their resulting vertical intervals (v_1 and v_2) within the three-part canons initiated in Ex. 123 can be seen in advance as demonstrated below:

Ex. 129

(a) $m = 1$, $v_1 = 5$
$v_2 = 8$

(b) $m = -2$, $v_1 = 4$
$v_2 = 9$

(c) $m = -3$, $v_1 = 3$
$v_2 = 10$

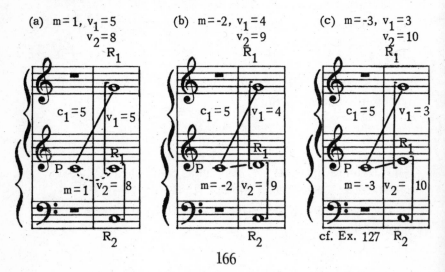

(d) $m=-4$, $v_1=2$
   $v_2=11$

(e) $m=-5$, $v_1=1$
   $v_2=12$

(f) $m=-6$, $v_1=-2$
   $v_2=13$

(g) $m=-7$, $v_1=-3$
   $v_2=14$

(h) $m=-8$, $v_1=-4$
   $v_3=15$

(i) $m=+2$, $v_1=6$
   $v_2=7$

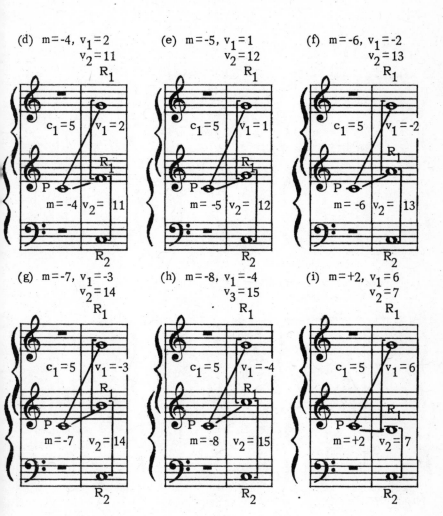

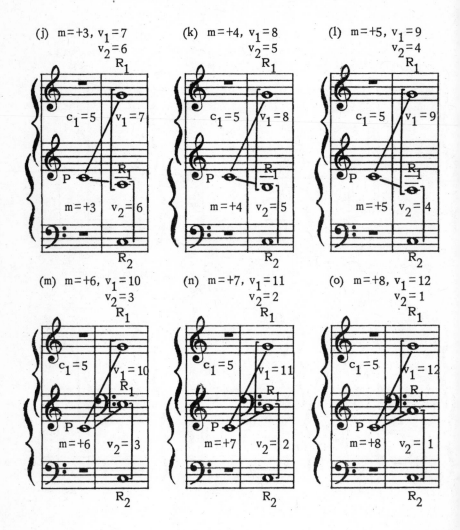

168

Which of these melodic intervals (m) together with their resulting v_1 and v_2 intervals are usable depends upon the harmonic and melodic textures that are desired. But, at whatever point in the canon a given m may occur, the resulting v_1 and v_2 will inevitably be the same.

11. In a three-part canon cast in entrance arrangements (5) and (6) as listed in paragraph 1 of Chapter VIII, the process is the same as that shown above through *Step three*. At *Step four*, however, things are done differently. In the following exposition no comments are necessary until *Step four*.

Step one:
   Ex. 130

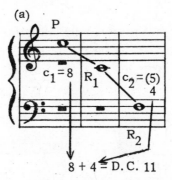

Step two:
   Ex. 130

Step three:
Ex. 130

(c)

Step four: Write on the remaining staff, the highest or lowest as the case may be, an imaginary note equal to the D. C. in force above or below R_1; and then transpose this note one octave (two octaves if necessary) inward towards R_1.

Ex. 131

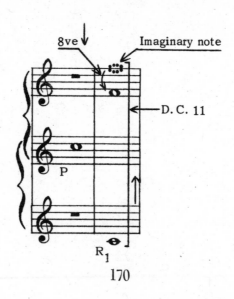

170

It is against the solid notes that m will be directed in order to determine in advance the intervals of v_1 and v_2.

Step five:

Ex. 132

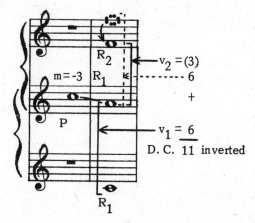

In v_2 the actual interval is that involving the solid note, while the addible interval is the one involving the imaginary note. From here on the available intervals are determined as is shown in Ex. 129.

12. From what is demonstrated above in paragraphs 8–11 it should now be clear that the success of a multi-voiced canon depends in large measure upon the constituent three-part canons being so planned that their respective m intervals produce complementary v_1 and v_2 intervals. Otherwise, an impasse can come about in which no melodic intervals will produce satisfactory vertical combinations. However, what combinations are usable depends upon the harmonic idiom in which the canon is cast. That is, a canon operating within pure triadic harmony will be less flexible melodically than one employing chords of the seventh and ninth, or non-triadic formations.

171

13.   When more than one c. u. separate the entrances of P and R_1, R_1 and R_2, R_2 and R_3, etc. depending upon the number of voices in the canon, the vertical alignment calculations operate precisely as shown in paragraphs 8 – 11 above except that each c. u. actually initiates a separate one c. u. three-part canon (cf. paragraph 12 in Chapter II). Ex. 133 proposes a three-part canon derived from D. C. 14 with each entrance separated by three c. u.

Ex. 133

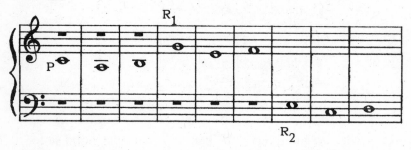

A problem such as the above can be most readily visualized as three interlocking single c. u. canons by connecting the corresponding c. u. by different kinds of lines thus:

     1st c. u. ──────
     2nd c. u. ────────
     3rd c. u. ....

This method of identification is shown in Ex. 134.

Ex. 134

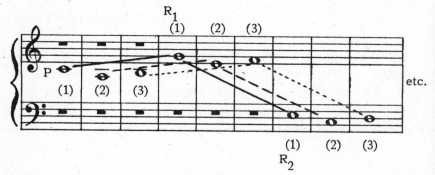

Thus, each c. u. can be calculated according to its own vertical alignment, so that the complete canon actually consists of three separate vertical alignments in operation simultaneously.

CANON WITH UNEQUALLY SPACED ENTRANCES

14.   No direct calculation process for constructing multi-voiced canons with unequally spaced entrances exists. Such canons operate in the form of the uncalculated three-part canons within a canon of four or more equally spaced entrances (cf. Ex. 115(b) in paragraph 1). Thus, by treating either R_1 or R_2 as imaginary voices–that is to say, silent–two three-part canons with unequally spaced entrances can be extracted from the four-part canon proposed in Ex. 115, thus:

Ex. 135

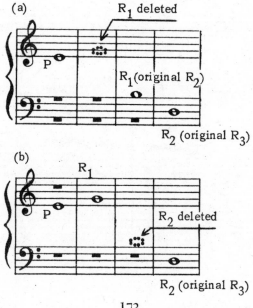

15. When the above two uncalculated three-part canons are extracted from the four-part canon in Ex. 118 they can, of course, be embellished in countless ways. Using the harmonic and linear texture as developed in Ex. 118, these are embellished as string trios in Ex. 136(a) and (b) below, the two treatments being unlike.

Ex. 136
(a) cf. Ex. 135 (a)

(b) cf. Ex. 135 (b)

175

16.   When a canon with unequally spaced entrances is to be extracted from a systematically constructed multi-voiced canon with equally spaced entrances, the problem can be treated in two ways:

   (1) the parts to be omitted operate in correct counter-point against the parts that are retained, or

   (2) the omitted parts need not operate in correct counterpoint against those that are retained since they will never be heard together.

The latter may make for greater linear freedom, both in the basic canon and in the embellishment.

17. Since a canon in four or more parts is merely an extension of the three-part canon principle, the Spiral Canon and Canonic Recurrence can be written in the usual manner. However, as the number of voices and the number of constituent three-part canons are correspondingly increased, the problem of making satisfactory connections become more difficult.

CHAPTER XI

CANON IN AUGMENTATION: CANON IN DIMINUTION

1.   A canon is in Augmentation when the R is in longer notes than those in the P,

Ex. 137

and in Diminution when the R is in shorter notes than those in the P.

Ex. 138

When R is the part in shorter notes (i. e. in a canon in diminution), a special problem comes about when it has progressed by as many c. u. as it follows the entrance of P in that the c interval occurs in two adjacent vertical intervals. Thus, a serious error would result if such a canon were written with c = 1, 5 or 8.

2. When the two parts begin simultaneously neither one serves as P or R, so that such a canon can be thought of as being either in augmentation or diminution.

Ex. 139

3. Embellishment, even though extremely modest, can greatly change the nature of a canon in augmentation. A seemingly inconsequential rhythmic elaboration in the P affects every aspect of the flow of the canon when it is augmented in the R. Ex. 140 shows a slightly embellished version of the canon beginning originally given above in Ex. 137.

179

Ex. 140

4. The part in longer notes can be related in any desired time proportion to the part in shorter notes. In the preceding illustrations the proportion is 2 : 1. Augmentation canons in the proportion of 3 : 1 and 4 : 1 could begin as shown below and would be described as canons in Triple Augmentation and Quadruple Augmentation respectively.

Ex. 141

(a) Canon in Triple Augmentation

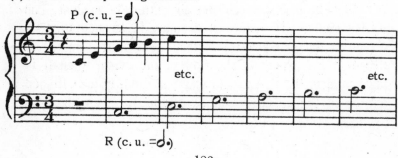

(b) Canon in Quadruple Augmentation

P (c. u. = ♩)

R (c. u. = 𝐨)

5.   Likewise, the augmentation may be in any other desired proportion, such as 3 : 2, 4 : 3, 5 : 3, 8 : 5, etc. However, because such canonic structures are usually merely imitations and do not generally involve any repeats, these will not be taken up here. But, the repeat processes that will be discussed in the remainder of this chapter can, is desired, be applied to these more involved proportions without further explanation.

6.   To deal most efficiently with the repeat problem in a canon in augmentation and to avoid unnecessary verbiage, the following code of identifications is being established for use in the remainder of this chapter:

P – the part in short notes, regardless of its point of entrance in relation to the part in longer notes.

R – the part in longer notes.

1, 2, 3, etc.–the c. u. numbering in P.

1, 2, 3, etc.–the c. u. numbering in R.

7.   The present repeat problem concerns that of making the P repeat while R is being heard only once. When the augmentation is in the proportion of 2 : 1, the P will be played twice against the R once. Ex. 142 demonstrates this problem solved in extremely simple terms.

Ex. 142

The above canon in its entirety will not repeat successfully insomuch as the two terminal intervals are unisons,
thereby bringing about an unsatisfactory progression—consecutive unisons—at the repetition. Thus, a free coda is
required to conclude the canon satisfactorily. Should the
entire mechanism be repeatable, the canon must be constructed at an interval that produces an acceptable progression when two are played successively, such as 3rds
or 6ths.

8.   To compose a canon like that in Ex. 142, proceed
as follows:

Step one: Determine the desired length in terms of c. u.,
and number same according to the system established in
paragraph 6. This will preclude the possibility of confusion
in the intervallic calculations.

182

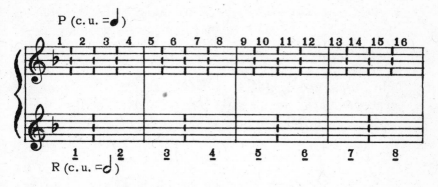

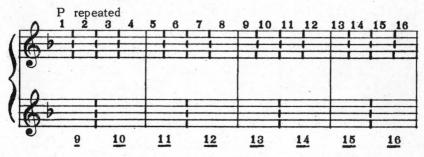

From the above diagram it will be seen that numerous double counterpoint situations come into play in that every pair of c. u. in the P will be pitted against two different c. u. in the R, as follows:

    1 2 operate against 1 and 9
    3 4 operate against 2 and 10
    5 6 , operate against 3 and 11
    7 8 operate against 4 and 12
    9 10 operate against 5 and 13
    11 12 operate against 6 and 14
    13 14 operate against 7 and 15
    15 16 operate against 8 and 16

183

The interval between the two c. u. in the R, against which a given pair of c. u. in the P operates, determines the D. C. inversion in force in that particular situation. For instance, in Ex. 142 the interval between 1 (F) and 9 (C) is a 5th. Thus, 1 and 9, the notes that are shifted vertically, relate to 1 2 in D. C. 5 (D. C. 12–8).

Step two: Write in the first and last notes in the two occurrences of P and in the one of R.

Ex. 144

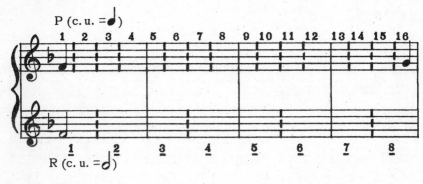

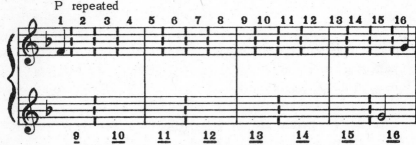

Step three: Fill in suitable notes in the vacant c. u. until the canon is completed as in Ex. 142. It is necessary to be continually cognizant of the double counterpoint situations occasioned by the numerical relationships tabulated

184

under Ex. 143. The order in which the c. u. are filled in will undoubtedly vary from one canon to another, but it is generally expedient to alternate the process from the middle, the beginning and the end; and not attempt to insert a continuous line from one end to the other. Actually, in completing Ex. 142, the filling in was begun by inserting c. u. 2, 15, 8 and 9 in that order.

Ex. 145

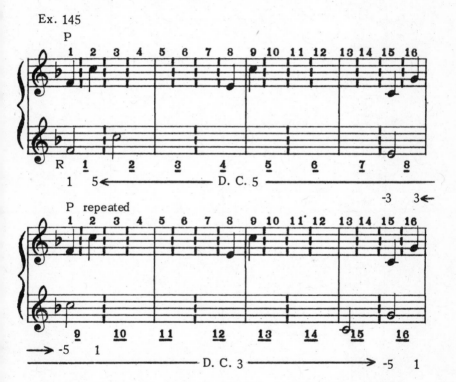

With this much of a start provided, it is left to the student to continue *Step three* until the canon as given in Ex. 142 is completely reconstructed. Also, the double counterpoint involvements for the entire canon can be identified as shown below.

185

Ex. 146

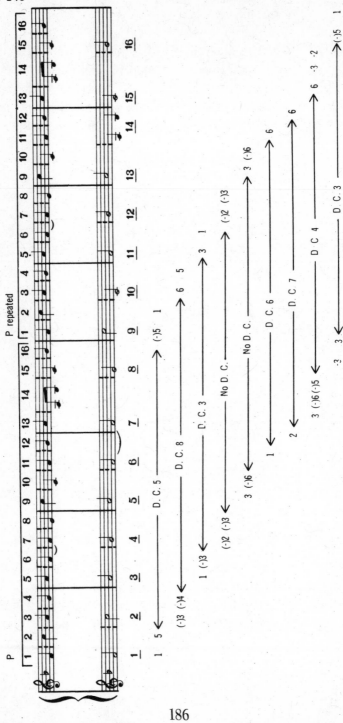

186

Where the minus sign is in parenthesis (–) it merely signifies that the P comes below the R and does not figure into the inversion. When the minus sign is *not* enclosed in parenthesis, it does figure into the D. C. calculations. The latter condition exists when the P crosses the R within the c. u.

9.   Embellishment in the form of melodic elaboration is as good as impossible in a canon in augmentation, due to the fact that structurally inconsequential fast notes in the P would, when augmented in the R, bring about all sorts of contrapuntal complications (cf. Ex. 140). However, some embellishment can be achieved through phrasings and chromatics. Two different versions of the canon developed in Ex. 142 – 146, each closing with a short coda, follow.

Ex. 147

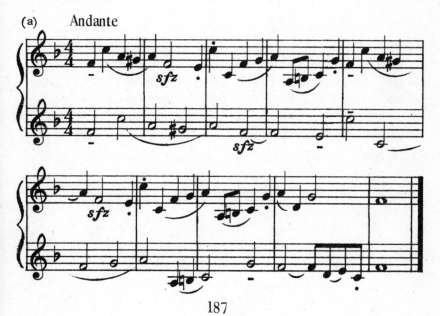

(b)

Andante

10. A canon in triple augmentation is constructed in much the same way as a canon in double augmentation. Only one mechanical restriction must be observed: should the canon be at the unison, 5th or 8ve, the P and R should not contain an even number of c. u. because at the exact middle the two parts would unavoidably progress by consecutive unisons, 5ths or 8ves respectively. In Ex. 148 is given, complete with D. C. calculations, an example of a canon at the 6th in triple augmentation, P in I. v. and with 15 c. u. in the theme. Further explanation of the process is unnecessary.

188

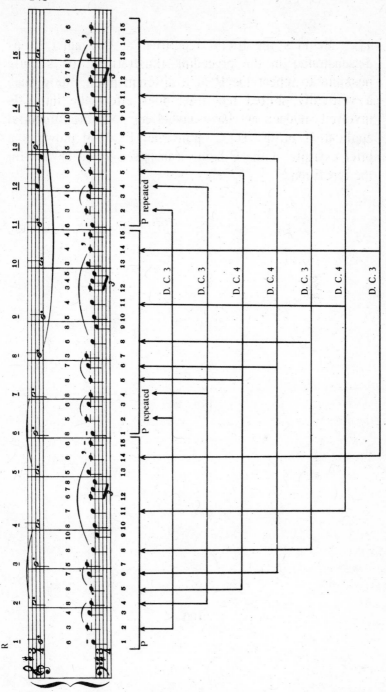

Ex. 148

189

11.   Besides the literal repetition of P against R, as demonstrated in the preceding illustrations, it is quite possible to repeat the P at a different pitch. While such a vertically shifted repetition does affect the intervals involved, it does not have any effect upon the structural application of the D. C. principle. Ex. 149 provides a brief example of the P being transposed a 2nd upward for the repetition.

Ex. 149

191

The above canon with the addition of very slight chromatic embellishment, a few phrasing indications, and a brief coda could appear as given below in Ex. 150. The tied quarter-notes in the P are here written as syncopated half-notes, which changes nothing audibly.

Ex. 150

12.　Numerous possibilities exist for composing distinctive augmentation canons in which the repetition of the P and/or the R appear either in contrary motion, in retrograde, or in contrary motion combined with retrograde. Ex. 151 shows a simple illustration wherein the P is repeated in retrograde and the R is written in contrary motion to the original P. Here the D. C. calculations must be figured in retrograde in the latter half of the canon as the arrows indicate.

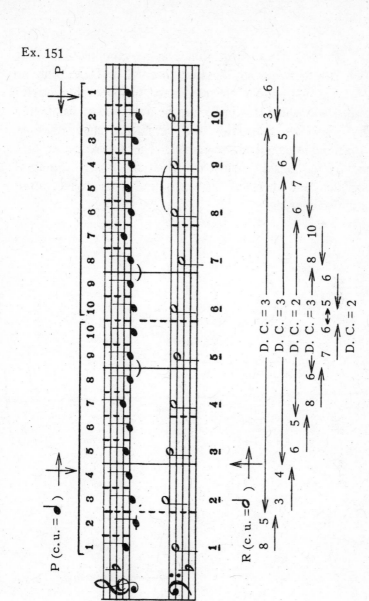

193

13.   Canons in augmentation can be constructed so as to be invertible at any desired interval of D. C., but no additional instructions are necessary. Considerably greater freedom and added flexibility can be achieved by employing more dissonant harmonies and permitting more liberties in the contrapuntal dissonances. The examples in this chapter are meant simply to illustrate basic structural principles and therefore use only the most conservative textural resources.

CHAPTER XII

THE ROUND

1.　When viewed as a canon type, the Round can be defined thus: a multi-voiced canon at the unison, with equally spaced entrances, and having the same number of c. u. between the double bars as there are between each pair of successive entrances. The following example by Haydn shows these conditions in operation.

Ex. 152

Tod und Schlaf

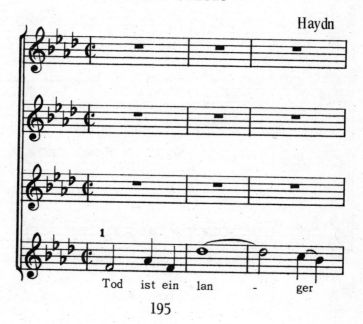

195

Tod ist ein lan - ger

Schlaf, Schlaf ist ein kur-zer, kur-zer

Tod ist ein lan - ger

Schlaf, Schlaf ist ein kur-zer, kur-zer

Tod. Die Not, die lin-dert der, und je-ner tilgt die

*) The point at which the round will end after it has been repeated as many times as may be desired

Any resemblance of a round to a canon lies solely in the manner of performance and not at all in the technical construction of the composition.

2. Structurally a round is simply a harmony in as many parts as may be desired, all within the range of a single voice, and being so planned that the end of each line flows smoothly into the first note of the next. The last line, for purposes of repeating effectively, will lead to the beginning of the first line. Thus, the compositional procedure would logically take place as follows:

Step one: Determine the number of parts required, the length of the parts, and the first and last note of each part.

197

Ex. 153

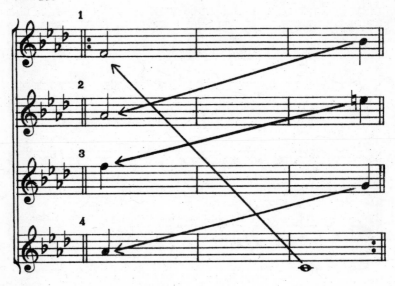

Step two: Complete the round by "filling in" suitable material in each line so that the entire composition becomes a unified and continuous melody that generates its own harmony, as is done in the last three measures of Ex. 152. The parts comprising the harmony may be as square-cut or as florid as artistic considerations dictate.
3. A pleasant means of diversion as well as a good exercise in melodic and harmonic invention can be had by taking the round format shown in Ex. 153, in this case it being Haydn's own plan, and completing it in different ways. Another solution to the above round problem by Haydn is attempted by the author in Ex. 154. While Haydn's familiar solution as given in Ex. 152 is of the utmost simplicity, the following endeavor is somewhat more com-

198

plex from almost every point of view. This is not to imply
that complexity is a virtue. Simplicity often is the greater
achievement. From a purely technical standpoint, however,
textural control–both linear and vertical–is the great
objective.

Ex. 154

CHAPTER XIII

CANONIC HARMONY

1.   Quite apart from its function as a contrapuntal composition, a canon may serve an entirely different purpose;
namely, as a kind of framework for organizing the sequence
of progressions within a harmonization. This can take
place in two general ways:

   (1)   by the addition of free voices below, above,
        within, or around a two-part canon, and
   (2)   by utilizing the harmonies rhythmically and
        functionally as they are determined by the
        restricted voice-leadings in a canon of three
        or more parts, although independently of the
        canonic lines.

Thus, canonic harmony–as a structural technique–differs
from free harmony in that its direction and content is
controlled mechanically. Because a canon so used is
often concealed, it is not always readily detected through
the usual harmonic analysis methods. Therefore canonic
harmony, as opposed to free harmony, may easily pass
unnoticed–either visually or audibly–by anyone who is
not skilled in canon and its varied and often quite elusive
uses.

2.   Many chorale harmonizations are constructed on this
principle. Ex. 155(a), (b) and (c) demonstrate three different
kinds of canons employed in this way. In each illustration,
the canon is extracted from the harmonization and subjoined to it.

Ex. 155

Bach, "Komm, heiliger Geist, Herre Gott"
line 3

(a)

Cf. Chapter II

(b)

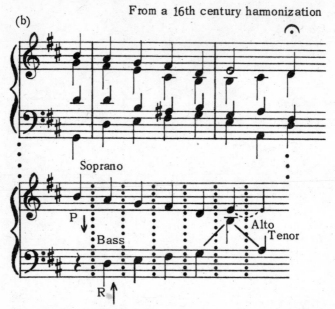

Cf. Chapter V, paragraphs 12 – 13, repeat not carried out.

Bach, "Wer nur den lieben Gott lasst walten"
(c)   line 2

Cf. Chapter VI

202

3.   The entire Preludio I of the Well-Tempered Clavier, Volume I, by Bach is composed in this way. Texturally, except for the three last measures, this 35-measure movement consists of a five-part harmony arpeggiated into two identical eight-note figures per measure, thus:

However, when written as chords it can be seen that the harmony is built around two two-part canons that overlap at the middle of the composition. The two canons are delineated by .... and ────── respectively. The double bars do not indicate any performance repetition, merely the mechanics of the first canon. The second canon merely dissolves without any calculated repeating structure.

Ex. 157.

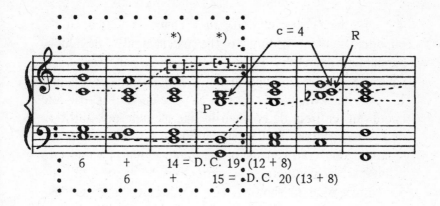

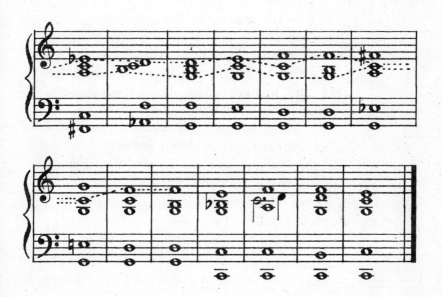

*) Notes in parenthesis in harmony, but at a lower octave.

4.   As the number of parts in a canon is increased the opportunities for adding to the mechanically developed harmonies diminish. Thus, in the three-part canons in Chapters VIII and IX and in those in four parts in Chapter X, the harmonies–except for an occasional incomplete chord–are entirely determined by the melodic possibilities of the mechanism. In Ex. 89 in Chapter VII, wherein two simultaneous crab canons in contrary motion combine into a four-part harmonization, no options exist.

5.   From what is shown it can be deduced that the composition of artistically valid canonic harmony calls into play a three-fold technique:

   (1)   the selection and control of a canon type that will produce a harmonic fabric to meet the artistic requirements of the composer,
   (2)   the ability to add other parts to the mechanical structure to bring about the desired kind and quality of harmonic energy, and
   (3)   skill in modulation and chromaticization to make the harmony as colorful and active as may be necessary to suit the composer's purposes.

All three aspects of the canonic technique in harmony are demonstrated with consummate virtuosity in the Bach Preludio shown in Ex. 156 – 157.

CHAPTER XIV

EMBELLISHMENT

1.   From the purely creative point of view, embellishment may well be the most communicative aspect of canon writing. While any competent mechanic can construct a canon once he has learned the intervallic technique, it takes an artist to transform it into a musical composition by means of embellishment. Thus, what follows–namely, the categorization of the art of embellishment into five elementary techniques that are applicable singly or in combination–may at first seem to be an oversimplification. For the present purposes of illustration the extremely simple canon in Ex. 22 in Chapter II will serve as model.

2.   *First embellishment technique:* rhythmic variation

Ex. 158 (see Ex. 22)

No notes other than those appearing in the basic outline canon (Ex. 22) are used in this rhythmically embellished version.

3. *Second embellishment technique*: auxiliary-notes, passing-notes, appoggiaturas, etc. in the same register as the outline canon

Ex. 159 (see Ex. 22 and cf. Ex. 158)

1) Auxiliary-note
2) Passing-note
3) Appoggiatura

4. *Third embellishment technique:* involving other notes
of the harmony

Ex. 160

(a) Basic outline canon (cf. Ex. 22) plus other notes of harmony.

Other notes of the harmony in combination with the first and
(b)   second embellishment techniques.

☐ Basic canon notes

⠿ Other notes of the harmony

Unmarked notes: Discords as used in the second embellishment technique.

210

5. *Fourth embellishment technique:* shift of selected notes in the basic canon up or down an octave.

Ex. 161

(a) Basic outline canon with selected notes shifted (cf. Ex. 22).

(b)

A measure by measure comparison of the above with Ex. 161(a) and with Ex. 22 will show at a glance how this version of the canon is derived.

6. *Fifth embellishment technique*: extension of the notes of the basic canon into ties, suspensions and retardations.

Ex. 162

Two other versions of this canon are given in Ex. 24(a) and (b).

7. Herewith is demonstrated in the simplest possible terms the five basic embellishment processes which in combination with chromaticization—either ornamental or modulatory—can be developed into an adequate technique for use in canon writing.

INDEX

215

216